# Southern Africa

*Southern Africa* surveys the contemporary history of the whole region encompassing economic, social, political, security, foreign policy, health, environmental and gender issues in one succinct volume.

Positioning the collapse of Portugal's African empire in the context of the region's history since 1945, Farley asserts that this led to the rapid transfer of power from minority to majority in Angola and Mozambique and more gradual transition in Zimbabwe, Namibia and South Africa. He examines the experiences of these countries as well as the former High Commission territories of Swaziland, Botswana and Lesotho to analyse the kind of states that evolved and shows how Southern Africa's present problems are the inevitable result of a long history of White rule. The book assesses the challenges faced by Southern Africa's political leaders up to the present day and discusses how these problems might be successfully addressed in the future.

With maps, a chronology and a glossary of acronyms, this is a valuable resource for all those interested in African history, politics and culture.

**Jonathan Farley** worked in the Department of History and International Affairs at the Royal Naval College, Greenwich, teaching mainly African and Middle East politics on naval officer courses. He retired in 1999.

# The Making of the Contemporary World
Edited by Eric J. Evans and Ruth Henig

The Making of the Contemporary World series provides challenging interpretations of contemporary issues and debates within strongly defined historical frameworks. The range of the series is global, with each volume drawing together material from a range of disciplines – including economics, politics and sociology. The books in this series present compact, indispensable introductions for students studying the modern world.

**Asylum Seekers and Refugees in the Contemporary World**
*David J. Whittaker*

**China Under Communism**
*Alan Lawrence*

**The Cold War**
*David Painter*

**Communism and Its Collapse**
*Stephen White*

**Conflict and Reconciliation in the Contemporary World**
*David J. Whittaker*

**Conflicts in the Middle East since 1945**
*Beverley Milton-Edwards and Peter Hinchcliffe*

**Decolonization**
*Raymond Betts*

**Dividing and Uniting Germany**
*J. K. A. Thomaneck and Bill Niven*

**The Extreme Right in Western Europe**
*Paul Hainsworth*

**The International Economy since 1945**
*Sidney Pollard*

**Islamic Fundamentalism since 1945**
*Beverley Milton-Edwards*

**Latin America**
*John Ward*

**Pacific Asia**
*Yumei Zhang*

**The Soviet Union in World Politics**
*Geoffrey Roberts*

**States and Nationalism in Europe since 1945**
*Malcolm Anderson*

**Terrorists and Terrorism in the Contemporary World**
*David J. Whittaker*

**Thatcher and Thatcherism**
*Eric J. Evans*

**United Nations in the Contemporary World**
*David J. Whittaker*

**The Uniting of Europe**
*Stanley Henig*

**US Foreign Policy since 1945**
*Alan P. Dobson and Steve Marsh*

**Women and Political Power in Europe since 1945**
*Ruth Henig and Simon Henig*

# Southern Africa

## Jonathan Farley

Routledge
Taylor & Francis Group

LONDON AND NEW YORK

First published 2008 by Routledge
2 Park Square, Milton Park, Abingdon, Oxon OX14 4RN

Simultaneously published in the USA and Canada
by Routledge
270 Madison Ave, New York, NY 10016

*Routledge is an imprint of the Taylor & Francis Group, an informa business*

The right of Jonathan Farley to be identified as the author of this work
has been asserted by him in accordance with the Copyright, Designs and
Patents Act 1988

Typeset in Times New Roman by
The Running Head Limited, www.therunninghead.com
Printed and bound in Great Britain by
TJ International Ltd, Padstow, Cornwall

*British Library Cataloguing in Publication Data*
A catalogue record for this book is available from the British Library

*Library of Congress Cataloging in Publication Data*
Farley, Jonathan.
Southern Africa / Jonathan Farley.
    p.   cm. — (The making of the contemporary world)
    Includes bibliographical references and index.
1. Africa, Southern—History—1975–   2. Africa, Southern—History—1899–1975.
I. Title.
DT1165.F37 2008
968—dc22             2007031609

ISBN10: 0–415–31034–2 (hbk)
ISBN10: 0–415–31035–0 (pbk)
ISBN10: 0–203–41618–X (ebk)

ISBN13: 978–0–415–31034–5 (hbk)
ISBN13: 978–0–415–31035–2 (pbk)
ISBN13: 978–0–203–41618–1 (ebk)

Dedicated to the memory of
Cynthia Kathleen Farley
1945–2005

# Contents

# Illustrations

**Maps**

**Figure**

# Acknowledgements

This book has been in preparation and execution for some eight years and during this time I have received much help and support, which I now acknowledge most warmly. My first debt is to the Winston Churchill Memorial Trust – and especially its then director-general, Sir Henry Beverley – for facilitating my journey to Southern Africa in 1994–5 by awarding me a travelling research fellowship. Over almost two months, I visited Namibia, Zimbabwe, Swaziland and South Africa and adduced much valuable information about the political, economic and social configuration of these countries and indeed of Southern Africa generally. My thanks are also due to Professor Geoffrey Till and my former colleagues at the then Royal Naval College, Greenwich for coping so ably and cheerfully with my absence.

Work commitments then prevented me from embarking on this book until after my retirement in 1999, but eventually, in 2003, Routledge agreed to accept this title into their 'Making of the Contemporary World' series and I have been grateful for both their initial confidence and continuing support in the years since. A further visit to the region in 2006 (this time limited to South Africa) enabled me to update some of the impressions gained 11 years previously.

Both academic colleagues and personal friends have been unstinting in their advice and support. I would pay a particular tribute to Professor Jack Spence, who has been involved with this work since its inception and devoted more time to reading first and second drafts than I had any right to expect, and without whose general encouragement and support I do not think I could have coped. I am also most grateful to Dr Heather Deegan, Professor James Barber and Mr William Turner (formerly British high commissioner in Botswana) who have all given me similar willing help and guidance. I am much indebted to old personal friends, John and Sylvester Smith and Judy and Richard

Burnett-Hall, for loaning me the peace and quiet of their homes to cogitate and write.

My late wife, Cynthia, to whom I am proud to dedicate this book, typed the first part of the script. After her tragic death in 2005, this task was most ably completed by Mrs Christine Groom, who coped most valiantly with my sometimes indeterminate handwriting and intermittent 'endnote confusion' from her home in Norfolk. The six maps are the work of Vinnie Powell, to whom I am much indebted, and finally I would like to thank my brother Clive Farley for his rapid typing of the index and unstinting fraternal support. There are also many in South and Southern Africa, too numerous to list in full, who gave most generously of their time and advice and to whom I remain most grateful. I thank each and every one of the foregoing for the contribution they made in bringing this work to fruition. The errors that remain, alas, are mine and mine alone.

Jonathan Farley
June 2007

# Glossary of acronyms

| | |
|---|---|
| ANC | African National Congress |
| APGRM | African Peer Group Review Mechanism |
| ASGI | Accelerated and Shared Growth Initiative |
| AU | African Union |
| BCP | Basuto Congress Party |
| BCP | Botswana Congress Party |
| BDP | Botswana Democratic Party |
| BNF | Botswana National Front |
| BNP | Basutoland National Party |
| BOSS | Bureau of State Security |
| BSAC | British South Africa Company |
| CC | Constitutional Court |
| CHOGM | Commonwealth Heads of Government Meeting |
| COSATU | Confederation of South African Trade Unions |
| DA | Democratic Alliance |
| DC | Congress of Democrats |
| DRC | Democratic Republic of Congo |
| DTA | Turnhalle Democratic Alliance |
| ECOWAS | Economic Community of West African States |
| EC | European Community |
| EEC | European Economic Community |
| ESKOM | Electricity Supply Commission |
| EU | European Union |
| FAA | Forças Armadas Angolanas |
| FF | Freedom Front |
| FNLA | National Front for the Liberation of Angola |
| FRELIMO | Front for the Liberation of Occupied Mozambique |
| G8 | The eight principal member states of the OECD |
| GEAR | Growth, Economic and Redistribution Plan |

| | |
|---|---|
| HIV/AIDS | Human immunodeficiency virus/acquired immune deficiency syndrome |
| IFP | Inkatha Freedom Party |
| INM | Imbokodvo National Movement |
| LCD | Lesotho Congress for Democracy |
| MDC | Movement for Democratic Change |
| MPLA | Popular Movement for the Liberation of Angola |
| NATO | North Atlantic Treaty Organisation |
| NCA | National Constitutional Assembly |
| NEPAD | New Plan for African Development |
| NIBMAR | No Independence before Majority African Rule |
| NNLC | Ngwane National Liberation Congress |
| NP | National Party |
| OAU | Organisation of African Unity |
| OECD | Organisation for Economic Co-operation and Development |
| OPDS | Organisation on Policy, Defence and Security |
| PAC | Pan-African Congress |
| PUDEMO | People's United Democratic Movement |
| RDP | Renewal and Development Plan |
| RENAMO | National Resistance Movement for Mozambique |
| SACP | South African Communist Party |
| SACU | South African Customs Union |
| SADC | Southern African Development Community |
| SADCC | Southern African Development Co-ordinating Conference |
| SADF | South African Defence Forces |
| SFTU | Swazi Federation of Trade Unions |
| SONANGOL | Angolan National Fuels Company |
| SWAPO | South West African People's Organisation |
| SWAYCO | Swazi Youth League |
| TRC | Truth and Reconciliation Commission |
| UANC | United Africa National Congress |
| UDI | Unilateral Declaration of Independence |
| UDM | United Democratic Movement |
| UNAVEM | United Nations Angola Verification Bureau |
| UNITA | National Union for the Total Independence of Angola |
| UNOMOZ | United Nations (Peace) Operations in Mozambique |
| UNSC | United Nations Security Council |
| ZANU-PF | Zimbabwe African National Union Patriotic Front |
| ZAPU | Zimbabwe African People's Union |

| | |
|---|---|
| ZCC | Zimbabwean Council of Churches |
| ZCCJP | Zimbabwe Catholic Commission for Justice and Peace |
| ZCTU | Zimbabwe Congress of Trade Unions |
| Zimrights | Zimbabwe Human Rights Association |
| ZUJ | Zimbabwean Union of Journalists |
| ZUM | Zimbabwe Unity Movement |

# Outline chronology of main events

| | |
|---|---|
| *circa* 1460 | Initial European settlements (by Portuguese) in West Africa. |
| 1475 | Lagos founded. |
| 1480–1550 | Portuguese settle in Angola and Mozambique. |
| 1652 | First Dutch settlements in the Cape under Jan van Riebeeck of the Dutch East India Company. |
| 1700 | These settlements consolidated. Gradual expansion north and eastwards thereafter. |
| 1806 | First British arrivals at the Cape. |
| 1815 | End of Napoleonic Wars. Further British arrivals. |
| 1836–40 | Great Trek. |
| 1852–4 | Boer republics established in Transvaal and Orange Free State. |
| 1866 | Diamonds discovered at Kimberley. |
| 1877 | British invade Transvaal. |
| 1880–1 | First Anglo-Boer War. British defeated. |
| 1886 | Gold discovered on the Rand. Growing British pressure on these resources. |
| 1889 | C.E. Rudd's pioneer column enters Zambezia (later Rhodesia) under auspices of British South Africa Company. |
| 1890 | Salisbury (now Harare) founded. Rhodesia established as a territory of the British South Africa Co. |
| 1899–1902 | Second Anglo-Boer War. |
| 1902 | Boers defeated. Treaty of Vereeniging. South Africa reunified under British rule. Lord Milner's anglicisation policy. |
| 1906 | Election of Liberal government in UK. First attempt at Boer–British reconciliation. |

| | |
|---|---|
| 1910 | South Africa independent as British dominion (under minority rule). |
| 1912 | ANC established. |
| 1914–18 | First World War. South Africa belligerent on Britain's side. |
| 1919 | South Africa assumes control of German South West Africa under Versailles treaty. |
| 1923 | BSAC cedes control of Rhodesia to Britain. Rhodesia granted 'self-governing' colony status within British Empire. |
| 1948 | National Party election victory in South Africa. Apartheid era inaugurated. |
| 1953 | Central African Federation established. |
| 1960 | Sharpeville shootings. Harold Macmillan's 'wind of change' speech in Cape Town. |
| 1961 | South Africa leaves Commonwealth. |
| 1962 | ANC's policy of pacifism abandoned. Nelson Mandela declares 'armed struggle' the only way forward, subsequently arrested. First Bantustan, the Transkei, established. |
| 1963 | Demise of Central African Federation. |
| 1964 | Mandela sentenced to life imprisonment for high treason. Accession of Ian Smith's Rhodesian Front to power in Salisbury (April). Accession of Labour government in UK under Harold Wilson (October). |
| 1965 | Rhodesia's UDI. |
| 1966 | Implementation of UN sanctions on Rhodesian exports and oil embargo. In South Africa Hendrick Verwoerd assassinated, succeeded by J.B. Vorster. |
| 1974 | Military coup in Lisbon. Collapse of Portugal's African empire. |
| 1975 | Independence of Angola and Mozambique. Civil war breaks out in both countries. |
| 1976 | Soweto riots. Increase in guerrilla military activity against Rhodesia. |
| 1978 | Vorster resigns as prime minister. Succeeded by P.W. Botha. |
| 1979 | Lancaster House talks on future of Rhodesia. |
| 1980 | Independence of Rhodesia as Zimbabwe. |
| 1979–83 | Repeal of much 'petty apartheid' legislation. |
| 1983 | Botha's Trilateral Constitution. |

1985–8    Botha's 'Rubicon' speech. Increased upheaval in South Africa's townships thereafter.

1989    Botha's illness and his eventual replacement as president by F.W. de Klerk. Negotiations with the imprisoned Mandela commence.

1990    Release of Nelson Mandela. ANC, SACP and PAC legalised. Repeal of all apartheid legislation (completed early 1991).
Namibia independent under Sam Nujoma.

1992    End of civil war in Mozambique.

1994    South Africa achieves majority rule under Nelson Mandela.

1999    Thabo Mbeki succeeds Nelson Mandela as president of South Africa.

2000    Robert Mugabe defeated in constitutional referendum in Zimbabwe.

2002    Angolan civil war ends. Death of Jonas Savimbi.

2004    Thabo Mbeki returned for a second term as president with an enhanced majority.

2005    Hifikepunye Pohamba succeeds Sam Nujoma as president of Namibia.

2007    Jacob Zuma nominated as President of the ANC and is likely therefore to replace Thabo Mbeki as President of South Africa in 2009.

# Introduction

Perhaps no other continent than Africa has seen greater political change during the past half-century. When Queen Elizabeth II ascended the throne in 1952, only Liberia, Ethiopia, Libya and Egypt were ruled by people of Arab or African origin. By the end of the twentieth century, the whole of the continent had come under indigenous rule: indeed, even before the end of the 1950s, much of the Maghreb, Ghana and the Sudan had achieved statehood. These were followed early in the 1960s by the remaining British and French colonies in West and East Africa and by the vast territory of the Congo, the colonial preserve of Belgium. Only Portugal chose to defy the 'wind of change' which was by then blowing through the continent.

In Southern Africa, the pattern of European domination was rather different. Here the colonists were settlers, not, as pertained in most of Africa north of the Zambezi, administrators on contract. Like the indigenous inhabitants, they regarded these countries as their own. Their lives, emotions and aspirations were all bound up in these lands: both psychologically and financially, detachment was impossible. For the British in Nigeria, the French in Senegal and the Belgians in the Congo, detachment was perfectly possible because their lives were centred elsewhere – in Devon, Provence or Flanders as the case might be. They did not own or farm vast tracts of land, as did their counterparts in Southern Africa. Indeed, in many European colonies with the striking exception of Kenya, ownership of land by colonists was discouraged, if not indeed forbidden by law. In many, too, notably in West Africa, the climate was such as to render prolonged or permanent residence both unwise and unattractive with malaria and other tropical diseases a constant hazard.

None of this applied in the countries of Southern Africa. In most, the climate was benign and the anopheles mosquito, the carrier of malaria, did not operate with the same degree of efficacy and sometimes not at all. There was also no general bar on European land-ownership. To this situation of agreeable climate and permissive land-ownership must be added something which underpinned European prosperity throughout the region – the availability of a plentiful supply of cheap semi-skilled and unskilled Black labour. This enabled Europeans to enjoy a standard of living distinctly higher than their socio-economic counterparts on the continent of Europe.

At the outset, it is important to define 'Southern Africa'. Opinions on this differ, but I would define it as those countries which achieved majority rule after 1974 in the wake of the collapse of Portugal's African empire. This includes clearly Angola and Mozambique; it includes Zimbabwe, but excludes Zambia and Malawi, independent in 1964. It includes the former High Commission territories of Lesotho, Botswana and Swaziland, despite the fact of their independence during the 1960s, as geographic, economic and strategic reasons compel their inclusion in a regional consideration of Southern Africa. Finally it includes Namibia and South Africa, both of which threw off White rule more recently during the early to mid-1990s.

The present work will analyse two phenomena – firstly, the nature of White rule and White supremacy in Southern Africa and, secondly, the kind of states which have evolved since its demise and the problems and challenges they now face. Whilst the emphasis will be on this latter aspect rather than the former, the current situation in Southern Africa can only be understood through an appreciation of the region's past. This book will attempt to give a balanced view of both.

The story of Southern Africa, as told here, begins in the late 1940s and ends on the turn of the twentieth century to the twenty-first. The collapse of Portugal's African empire in the mid-1970s constitutes a watershed, for it set in train a pattern of events which were eventually to undermine the very foundations of White rule and create a series of polities very different from those which had gone before. Firstly, it shifted the frontiers of Black majority rule hundreds of miles further south and reinvigorated African nationalism as a political force. Secondly, it encouraged the Black populations of Rhodesia, Namibia and South Africa to think in terms of gaining political emancipation in the foreseeable rather than indefinite future. For politically aware Africans, the eclipse of Portuguese power appeared to sound the death-knell of White minority rule throughout the region. Whilst many struggles and much turmoil lay ahead, within six years Rhodesia had become independent under majority rule as Zimbabwe and within 15 South West Africa had thrown off the South African yoke and emerged as Namibia. The release of Nelson Mandela in February 1990 marked the start of a transition from minority to majority rule in South Africa, a transition completed by 1994 and more peaceful in nature than even the optimists of the day had dared to hope. Whether and to what extent South and Southern Africa can succeed in inspiring a similar spirit of optimism well into the twenty-first century is just one of the questions this book will attempt to answer.

# 1 The economic and social dimension

Europe's early motivation for involvement in Africa was primarily economic. The Portuguese were the first to arrive in Africa in the latter part of the fifteenth century and were concerned to trade, by leave of the local kings, in the commodities which the continent had to offer; by the early part of the sixteenth century they had built up a substantial pattern of trade across the Sahara Desert between Europe and the several kingdoms of West Africa. Various stretches of the West African coast were indeed named after the commodities in which this trade was conducted – the Ivory Coast, the Gold Coast and the Slave Coast. This trade, though initiated by the Portuguese, was later joined by the other powers of Europe and was, for 250 years after the middle of the sixteenth century, exceedingly profitable for all concerned, although the price of this was paid by Africans in terms of sheer brutality, enforced exile from their homeland and family separation. Not until the first part of the nineteenth century was this trade brought to an end but, sadly, by that time a pattern had been set for the treatment of Blacks by Whites which was to endure in a rather different form far into the twentieth century.

The 'Scramble for Africa' by the various powers of Europe began in the last quarter of the nineteenth century and involved a policy of both political and economic domination of almost the entire African continent. Before that time, the European presence was coastal and fragmented (see Map A): after 1875, the growth of European imperialism gave rise to mutual competition by its several powers for the largest and most economically significant territories available. A conference chaired by Otto von Bismarck was held in Berlin in 1884 to regulate this competition. By the eve of the First World War, this process was largely complete, Morocco being the last country to be divided between Spain and France in 1912 by the Treaty of Fez (see Map B, p. 6).

The position of Southern Africa must here be distinguished from its

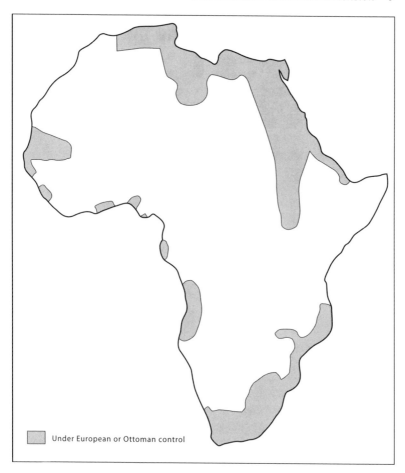

Under European or Ottoman control

*Map A* Africa in 1875 before 'the Scramble'.

Northern and Central counterparts. Except in Algeria where there had been a French presence since the 1830s, Northern and Central Africa had been largely free of European penetration until late in the nineteenth century. In Southern Africa, the Portuguese had made coastal settlements in contemporary Angola and rather later in Mozambique during the later fifteenth and mid-sixteenth centuries which they gradually expanded inland. By the middle of the seventeenth century, the Dutch under Jan van Riebeeck of the Dutch East India Company had made their first landings at the Cape and, by its end, had established settled farming communities as well as a rest and replenishment station for its

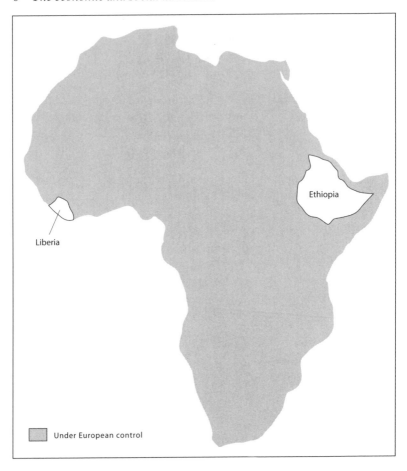

*Map B* Africa in 1912 after 'the Scramble'.

ships en route to the Dutch East Indies. During the eighteenth century these farming communities spread ever eastwards in search of land for grazing their cattle: this brought them increasingly into conflict with the Black tribes of the interior which were themselves moving in a south-westerly direction. The origins of Black–White conflict and, later, of White domination of Black are to be found in the competition between the races which occurred at this time. The Dutch needed, as indeed did the Portuguese in their territories further north, two things – access to land and access to a supply of unskilled labour. As a result of their dispossession at the hands of the Europeans, the Africans became the latter's serfs and this pattern of economic domination grew to be general throughout Southern Africa. This did not occur at once and there were numerous wars between Black and White, but essentially the former could not, in the final analysis, compete with the latter's superior technology. Thus the African became dominated by the European in the continent of his birth.

Whilst this was the general pattern throughout Southern Africa, a distinction must again be drawn between the areas in Portuguese hands and those in Dutch hands. In the former, there had been the practice of racial miscegenation from very early times: the early Portuguese colonists arrived in Africa without their womenfolk, the climate being then considered much too unhealthy for permanent residence by the fair sex. Therefore the colonists cohabited with the women of the continent, a practice which led over time to the creation of a mulatto population. In consequence, there was never the same degree of colour consciousness nor legal discrimination on grounds of race which occurred in the Dutch territories. Whilst Dutch farmers unquestionably had their sexual liaisons with Black women, these were carried on in a much more 'hole-and-corner' manner and ostensibly the ideal of Christian marriage and family life was preserved. Dutch immigrants to the Cape after 1652 did not come as single men but were accompanied by their wives and families and lived, at any rate on the surface, a life of monogamous self-denial according to the Calvinist dictates of the Dutch Reformed Church. Miscegenation was severely frowned upon and thus the social distinction between White and non-White was much more stark than that which pertained in Portuguese territory. But, in both Portuguese and Dutch Africa, there was no question of Africans being in a position other than one of subservience. For the Europeans, they were 'the sons of Ham'.

Portugal's colonial policy over the years varied in its degree of *dirigisme* depending on the strength and attitude of the government in power at the time. 'Settler power', however, was never as dominant a factor for Lisbon as it was for London in regard to Kenya and, most notably, Rhodesia. Angola and Mozambique were administered by a colonial governor appointed by Lisbon for a fixed term of office who kept himself apart from the Portuguese settler population and whose authority the latter was basically prepared to accept even if it had little means of influencing it. In Dutch Africa there was, apart from the Dutch East India Company, no outside authority to control the settlers, whose political power was thus paramount. This, combined with their messianic fervour to govern the country in accordance with God's will as they conceived it, to lead the non-Whites, however gradually, towards civilisation and spiritual salvation and to preserve all the while the ideals of their own Afrikaner identity, rendered them a highly conservative political force.

For a century and a half after arriving at the Cape and before the British influx in 1820 after the Napoleonic Wars, they developed untrammelled by the continent of Europe and immune from the ideas of the Enlightenment of the eighteenth century or the revolutionary upheavals of 1789 and after. By the time the British arrived, they were Dutch in name only. More accurately, they were White Africans.

But to move to the twentieth century: the first three decades of this witnessed considerable political instability in Portugal with numerous changes of government which caused a certain hiatus in the administration of her empire in Africa. Then, in 1928, Antonio de Salazar came to power in Lisbon and within a few years had made himself the undisputed master of the country. This 'new state' doctrine of 1933, essentially a highly centralised and authoritarian system of government based on that of Mussolini's Italy, was applied both in Portugal and in Portuguese Africa with full rigour. For Africans, this meant a system of contract labour, whereby they worked compulsorily for six months every year for a European employer and only after this could they undertake work on their own account. The assumption was that the African was inherently lazy and needed to be taught the 'civilising influence' of work; in practice the policy assured the European settler population of a ready supply of cheap labour. Africans were only exempt from this if they had previously achieved *assimilado* status; in other words, become sufficiently educated to write and speak Portuguese to secondary-school standard and to repeat their catechism. As most Africans in the Portuguese empire were entirely illiterate, the demands of the contract labour system were virtually universal. This bound Africans irretrievably into the European economic system, either as agricultural labourers or as miners in the diamond fields, and their contracts limited their ability to be in any way 'self-starting' for the duration. Even when the contract was over for the year, there was always next year. Wages were fixed by individual European employers at the lowest rate possible and it was hardly surprising if all those who could emigrated to Rhodesia or South Africa to find work where wages were higher, notwithstanding the racial discrimination which occurred in both countries.

Rhodesia, a territory of the British South Africa Company until 1923, became part of the British Empire in that year and was granted 'self-governing' status as Southern Rhodesia. The rationale behind this was that the country had some 30,000 Whites in residence and was in consequence sufficiently advanced to govern itself. The franchise was a heavily qualified one and very few Africans had the vote. Whilst certain key matters, notably foreign policy and constitutional issues, were reserved to Westminster and Whitehall, the latter were broadly pre-

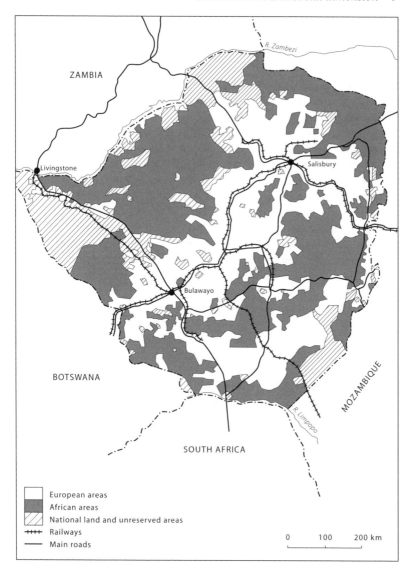

*Map C*  Rhodesia, showing land apportionment.

pared to leave everything else for the determination of the government in Salisbury. There thus grew up, after 1923, an economic and social system which was distinctly weighted in favour of the White minority. African influx to the main towns became regulated, Salisbury becoming a White city as early as 1929. The early 1930s saw the first of the Land Apportionment Acts which were to become an enduring feature of the country's economic fabric (see Map C, p. 9). These involved the designation of areas throughout the country in which Whites and non-Whites might own and occupy land. The most fertile land and that closest to lines of communication was reserved for White occupation and the remainder, approximately half, for non-White. Thus the African majority, which numbered some 673,000 at the time, was expected to occupy some 50 per cent of the land, whilst the White minority, consisting of but 35–40,000, were allocated the other 50 per cent.

It was not only over land that there was discrimination. For both Black and White communities, there were different pay scales for identical work. In the chrome mines, for example, these differed by a factor of ten and in other industrial and agricultural spheres they differed also, although here the discrepancy was rather less marked. The whole system was intentionally, and indeed legislatively, constructed to enable Whites to enjoy a way of life suitable to their civilisation, culture and religion and to bar the way for Blacks to this charmed circle.[1] It must not be forgotten that the White way of life in Southern Rhodesia depended on the availability of African labour which was both plentiful and cheap. This fact did not deter Africans from Northern Rhodesia, Nyasaland or the Portuguese colonies from coming to seek work there because wage levels in these places were yet more depressed. Southern Rhodesia indeed had gained a reputation amongst Africans by the mid-1930s for being 'a good place in which to work but a bad place in which to live', good because of high wage levels but bad because of the discriminatory laws, such as those on land apportionment and urban influx, which restricted the economic and social freedom of Africans in numerous ways. This broad policy became even more comprehensive after the formation of the Central African Federation in 1953, when the two Colonial Office territories of Nyasaland and Northern Rhodesia were incorporated along with Southern Rhodesia into one country. This move was extremely unwelcome to African nationalist opinion generally because they feared, not unnaturally, that the social discrimination which had for so long been practised in Southern Rhodesia would become the norm throughout the Federation. Events were subsequently to prove them right.

In South Africa itself, a similar pattern of White discrimination in the economic and social fields was established following independence under a minority-rule constitution in 1910. Given the denial of voting rights to Africans, there was no need for the White government in Pretoria to make any concessions to their grievances. The Mines and Works Act of 1911 and the Native Land Act of 1913 both wrote discrimination on grounds of race into the political system implicitly if not explicitly, and, indeed, a further act was needed in 1926[2] to assert that it had been the intention of the government to 'cap' the level to which Africans could rise in the mine hierarchy and, by the same token, the level of wage they could earn. The act of 1926 was brought in partly to ensure that 'responsible' positions in the mines would invariably be held by Whites and partly to eliminate the possibility of White unskilled miners becoming subordinate to Black foremen. Discrimination on grounds of race thus became for the first time both explicit and legal.

With the advent to power of the National Party in 1948, discrimination on racial grounds became the norm and ceased to be confined to particular statutes. The Native Labour Act of 1953 prevented Africans from joining existing (White) trade unions and deprived Africans of the right to strike for higher wages or better conditions of service. Perhaps the most draconian legislation of all, in the sense that it affected African life most directly, was the Native Laws Amendment Act of 1952 which was masterminded by Hendrick Verwoerd as minister of native affairs. This set rigid controls on the rights of Africans to live in urban areas: only if they had been born there, or lived there continually for 15 years, or worked there for the same employer for at least 10 years, could they be legally resident in White cities. If an African lost his job, he had but 72 hours to find another and, in default of this, was likely to be 'endorsed out' back to his tribal homeland. This statute was the more vicious in that it led to the break-up of families, for both man and wife had to qualify for residence: failure by either to do so would lead to one or other being exiled to his or her tribal homeland. Alister Sparks' comments in this regard are well worth perusing.[3]

After 1948, the Africans found their way blocked at virtually every turn. The Group Areas Act of 1950 gave the minister of native affairs power to designate that a piece of land be for occupation by a particular race only. This, over the years, led to the physical upheaval of established African communities and the mental distress occasioned for those affected is not difficult to imagine: people were shunted off to areas of which they had usually no knowledge and with which they had no connection. The Industrial Conciliation Act of 1956 likewise gave the minister of labour power to 'reserve' particular jobs for particular races, jobs involving close contact with the general public such as hotel or telephone receptionists being commonly 'reserved' for Whites. This, not infrequently, led to difficulties if there were insufficient members of the race concerned to fill the posts available and various stratagems and subterfuges had to be used in order to escape the consequences of the law. Nevertheless, the law remained in place, causing great inconvenience as well as extra expense to managers in factories and offices, not to mention frustration to non-Whites who were as often as not perfectly capable of doing the jobs from which they were legally excluded.

Why, it may be asked, was this situation, with all its anachronisms, allowed to develop? Essentially, this legislation had been passed to ensure the social and economic survival of the White community and, in particular, the Afrikaner component of it. With the industrialisation of South Africa which had occurred from the beginning of the twentieth century and the concomitant growth of South African cities, Whites found themselves coming into direct competition with Blacks for semi-skilled and unskilled work. In terms of education, they frequently had no more to offer than the Blacks, often being illiterate themselves. Employers thus tended to accept Blacks for employment as they were cheaper to employ than 'poor Whites' because, unlike the latter, they did not need to finance so high a standard of living. This, of course, was anathema to the White working class and led to the rise of 'civilised labour' policies which characterised South Africa from the 1920s onwards.[4] Government was compelled to respond to these White concerns through legislation to protect them, while for Blacks, who did not have to be appealed to because they did not have the vote, no response was necessary. The result, naturally, was the artificial buttressing of the Whites' economic position at the expense of the Blacks.

The term 'poor White' demands some further elaboration here. It relates to those Whites, both Afrikaners and English-speakers, whose standards of education and qualifications were poor or non-existent. Many Afrikaner peasant farmers, finding that they could no longer farm their smallholdings economically, were in this category and drifted into the cities from the beginning of the century onwards in search of unskilled, 'pick-and-shovel' work. This brought them into direct competition with the Africans who were in search of the same thing and very often better at it – they had been employed previously in this capacity on White farms, whereas the Whites had acted primarily as their overseers.

As in Rhodesia, a dual pay-scale system for White and non-White was established in South Africa; this walked hand-in-hand with the 'civilised labour' laws just referred to. It was simply not acceptable to the generality of the White population to rub shoulders with the non-White, a group they adjudged greatly inferior to themselves in any case, in search of unskilled work. They wanted protection from these hordes of primitive, uncivilised Black people who threatened to overwhelm them in respect of both employment and residence. The dual pay scale assured a measure of protection in this regard; the Industrial Conciliation Act of 1956 legally barred non-Whites from doing certain jobs and

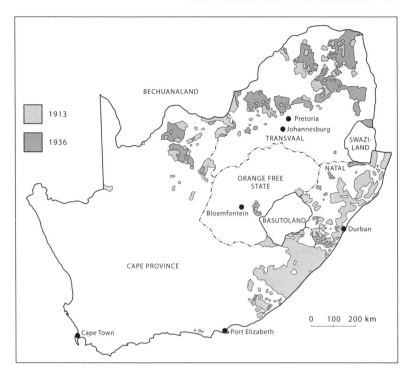

*Map D* African areas designated under the 1913 and 1936 Land Acts.

the Native Laws Amendment Act of 1952 regulated their employment in South Africa's main cities. In regard to residence, the Native Land Act of 1913 prevented Africans from owning land outside the Reserves (see Map D) and this restriction was fortified, in the early days of apartheid, by the Group Areas Act of 1950. The White government in Pretoria had created a prison for Black South Africans in the land of their birth.

Pretoria believed that this was essential if the White community was to preserve its own identity in the South African state. The inter-war period and, more specifically, the war period itself had seen a distinctive growth of the Black population and its increased presence in the cities, up from 139,000 in 1936 to 390,000 in 1948.[5] In 1955, Johannes Strijdom, by then prime minister, made this candid statement of policy in addressing a conference of the National Party:

> I am being as blunt as I can. I am making no excuses. Either the White man dominates in this country or the Black man takes over.

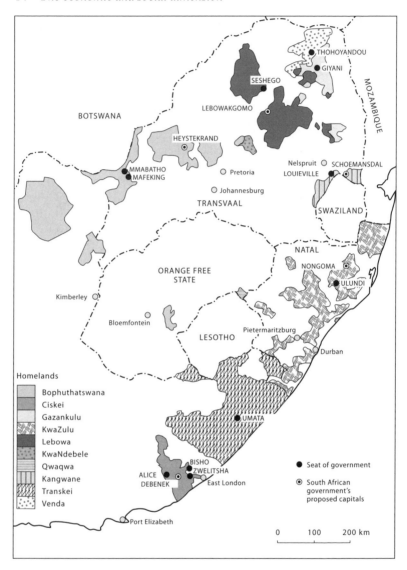

*Map E* Bantustans with the homeland capitals.

In practical terms, this meant a policy of *baaskap*, of White domination, and this was evinced in all spheres of government activity, including the economic. After 1958, however, this changed in form and presentation after the accession to the premiership of Hendrik Verwoerd.

Verwoerd was the most able and most active political thinker in the

National Party. Much of the key legislation of the early apartheid years bore his personal imprint. As minister of native affairs in the early 1950s he had also had practical experience of government. Though ideologically fanatical in terms of his belief in White supremacy, he was also sufficiently shrewd to appreciate the potential power of African nationalism and that a crude policy of *baaskap* would not be in the interest of White survival within South Africa. So, after acceding to the premiership in 1958, he came to talk about the importance of Blacks being able to 'realise themselves', to achieve their own political and cultural aspirations and to have sovereignty within their own traditional areas of residence. Thus the concept of the Bantustan was born, and the first of these was established in the Transkei by the Transkei Self Government Act of 1962. It was joined later in the 1960s and 1970s by others, Bophuthatswana, Lebowa and Venda among them (see Map E).

Broadly speaking, these African 'sovereign territories' were established in traditional areas of African residence, as laid down in the 1913 Native Land Act. Chiefly authority was important, but there was also to be provision for regular elections to local legislatures. Whites would be excluded from living in them and the hated pass laws, so ubiquitous in White South Africa, would not operate within them. Verwoerd's idea was that Africans would largely decamp from South Africa's principal cities (the preserve of the Whites) and go to live in the Bantustans, out of which they would commute every day to work in the White factories which would be established on their periphery. It would be government policy actively to support and financially to encourage this industrialisation process.

The Bantustans were duly established with their formal political infrastructures, but the problem was that the mass of the Africans did not wish to go and reside in them as Verwoerd had predicted. The reason for this was that the workplaces in the vicinity of the Bantustans never materialised despite the many attempts by government to encourage them. The Bantustans were themselves too remote from the traditional areas of industrial and economic activity and White entrepreneurs did not want to run the risk of making investments there. Consequently, Africans preferred to remain in their townships on the edge of the White cities, the pass laws notwithstanding, since it was there that they could most readily succeed in earning decent wages. The workless areas bordering the Bantustans held no enticement for them – with the result that Verwoerd's main objective of securing the work of the African but avoiding his physical presence in the White cities was not achieved. Verwoerd's policy represented a triumph of hope over reality: the traditional pattern of employment continued, African men working on contract in the White cities but living in the townships. The

Bantustans became areas inhabited primarily by their wives, children and old folk: the flower of the African workforce gravitated there only as temporary sojourners between contracts.

In concluding this economic survey of South Africa during the apartheid era, three points need to be made. Firstly, the country's whole economic structure had been artificially engineered over the years to give Whites 'a place in the sun'. This had led to great inefficiency and great expense due to job-reservation legislation, dual pay scales and employment protection. White salaries were as a rule disproportionately high and were correspondingly depressed for Blacks. Not always were there enough members of a particular race available to undertake work that needed to be done and the civil service represented, all too often, a jobs haven for 'poor Whites'. Secondly, the White economy could not have functioned at all without the labour of Africans in both mine and factory: to push the bulk of them into the Bantustans, as envisaged by Verwoerd, was not a policy which would have worked short of a wholesale restructuring of White industry away from its traditional locus. Thirdly, the racially discriminatory laws notwithstanding, the South African economy was by far the most wealthy and the most sophisticated in the whole of Southern Africa. It offered employment opportunities to Africans on a scale unknown within the several states bordering South Africa, and all this encouraged immigration on a large scale, which Pretoria, needing these labour units, did little to discourage. What it manifestly failed to do was to accept the premise that they too had some right to 'a place in the sun'; instead it confined them to a way of life which in no way reflected their ability, efforts or aspirations. The upheavals in the townships which began in 1976 and continued through to the end of the 1980s provide evidence enough of this. Notwithstanding the Botha reforms in the economic and industrial field of the 1979–84 period, which were substantial by South African standards,[6] these came too little and too late and did not in any material sense improve the lot of the average Black South African, who continued to see his White counterpart as permanently enjoying his privileged lifestyle. These reforms had raised African hopes without fulfilling them but thereby made Africans that more determined to come to share in European prosperity. It was that determination made so manifest in the township upheavals of the late 1980s combined with the barrenness of the governmental response to them which finally persuaded Pretoria that, though it might win battles defending apartheid, it could not, in the final analysis, win the war. It was this realisation that enabled Nelson Mandela to be released in February 1990 and for the dismantling of the apartheid state to follow soon afterwards.

However, neither the dismantling of apartheid in South Africa nor the termination of colonial rule in Zimbabwe and the former Portuguese territories spelt the end of Black–White economic inequality in Southern Africa. This inequality persists today and inevitably affects the political character of the region as a whole: this premise is fundamental to any analysis of Southern Africa's economic situation.

## Command and market economies

The most significant issue concerns the rejection of the 'command' for the 'market' economy. During the long period of White settler rule, capitalism became identified in the eyes of Blacks as the economic system of their oppressors. As long ago as 1955, the ANC recognised this in its 'Freedom Charter', Clause 3 of which spoke of the need to take the country's mineral resources, banks and monopoly industries into public ownership. Nelson Mandela denied in his autobiography that it was a socialist manifesto, asserting that it was only an anti-capitalist one in the context of getting rid of apartheid: it did not prohibit free enterprise per se. [7] Nor did it make any obeisance to Marxist-Leninist ideals, even if in subsequent years it was castigated for precisely that. However, after 1955, the new Soviet leadership gradually came to appreciate that African nationalism could, if properly handled, be harnessed as a force against capitalism and, in that sense, constitute a revolutionary force against the West in general. The 1950s, and more particularly the 1960s, saw the Soviet Union becoming more solicitous of the newly independent states of Africa, because it believed that their experience under colonial rule had made them endemically hostile towards the capitalist West and consequently favourably disposed towards the socialist East. Sékou Touré's Guinea, Kwame Nkrumah's Ghana and Julius Nyerere's Tanzania all serve to illustrate this: important diplomatic and economic linkages were established between the Soviet Union and these various states – to be followed by others as the 1960s turned into the 1970s, of which the Somalia of Siad Barre and the Zambia of Kenneth Kaunda are perhaps the most noteworthy.

In sum, the Cold War which had begun in Europe in the late 1940s was in subsequent decades, albeit at a much lower level, extended to Africa, whose newly independent states were lobbied for support by both West and East. The Soviet Union purported to demonstrate that it would do all in its power to alleviate the legacy of economic colonialism which continued to afflict the new states of Africa whilst the West was at pains, by way of offering favourable trade and aid arrangements, to ensure that these same states were not seduced by Soviet or Chinese blandishments. This was particularly true of France and her former colonies (with the notable exception of Guinea), and equally Britain was concerned to nurture the Commonwealth connection with such countries as Kenya and Nigeria. The US came to favour Zaire after 1965 because of Mobutu's staunch anti-Marxist stance. The situation became particularly brittle with the passage of time, partly due to Rhodesia's UDI in 1965 and the failure of either Britain or the international community to counter it, and partly due to the entry of the Soviet Union and Cuba in force into Angola and Mozambique in the mid-1970s. For the next ten years time seemed to be on the side of the Soviet Union, with centralised planning and 'command' economies being the order of the day.

All this changed after Mikhail Gorbachev's accession to supreme power in the Soviet Union in 1985. Gorbachev sought for the latter a completely new foreign policy and relationship with the Western world. He was unimpressed with his predecessors' support for African client states and for such indigenous movements as SWAPO in Namibia, which had cost the Soviet Union much money over the years but achieved little political good. His willingness to dismantle the Soviet–Cuban position in Angola in 1988 and his accommodation with the West in winding down the Iran–Iraq War in 1987 by way of Resolution 587 of the UN Security Council was indicative of this new Soviet attitude, an attitude which would have been inconceivable earlier in the decade. Only two years later, in 1989, the dismantling of the Berlin Wall and the rapid collapse thereafter of the Soviet empire in Eastern Europe gave Africa's politicians pause for thought. Were they wise, they argued, to persevere with 'command' economies when these were being rejected by the very states in which they originated?

Gorbachev believed that, if the USSR was to become an economic as well as a military superpower, it had to come to terms with the significance of market forces. It had to produce goods which people wanted to buy rather than expect them just to be content with whatever Moscow saw fit to dole out to them. These ideas, which he outlined in his book *Perestroika*, were revolutionary in their implications. Not since the 1917 Revolution had anyone seen their like.[8]

## The formal and informal sectors

For Southern Africa, the result was that central planning lost most of its earlier appeal. In Zimbabwe, President Robert Mugabe modified his economic intervention considerably after 1988 and the informal sector increased at the expense of the formal. In South Africa, after Nelson Mandela's accession to power in 1994, 'orthodox economic management' and regard for market forces prevailed over the state interventionism implicit in the Freedom Charter. There was a further reason for this over and above the events in Eastern Europe and the Soviet Union during the period 1989–91: many of the ANC leadership in exile abroad during the apartheid era had witnessed the failure of command economies in such countries as Zambia and Tanzania and did not wish to have similar failures repeated in South Africa. It was also made clear to the governments of Southern Africa by the World Bank and the International Monetary Fund that overseas investment was only likely to be forthcoming in significant quantities if they adopted 'orthodox procedures' in the implementation of their economic policies. This meant avoiding big budgetary deficits and keeping firm control of the money supply. Though this was done in South Africa and Namibia, the result has been a severe increase in the size of the informal sector and a decrease in the availability of stable employment. 'Structural adjustment policies' have also played a part, but more of this below.

At this point, a word must be said by way of definition of the 'formal' and 'informal' sectors. The former involves that part of the economy which is regulated either directly or indirectly by the state or by large public concerns associated with it, like ESKOM. Those employed in this area enjoy regular salaries (with which they can finance mortgages) and considerable stability of employment. It includes members of the professions as well as civil servants. By contrast, the 'informal sector' has none of this stability. Every month, indeed every week, is a period of financial uncertainty and the vast majority of Black Africans throughout the region find themselves in this situation; in South Africa, only 38 per cent of the Black population succeed in finding employment within the formal sector. The remaining 62 per cent are either on short contracts or piece-work in agriculture or mining, or scratch a living as best they can as taxi drivers, hair-cutters, street traders or vehicle breakers. With these activities, both their income and their continuous employment are uncertain, and when times are bad they rely on their families to make ends meet. The sheer size of the informal sector is mainly responsible for the continuing Black–White economic disparity as well as for the inability of the inland revenue authorities to gather in all the taxation monies which are due to them, given that so many of the transactions which occur are on a cash basis and individual liabilities are hence difficult to gauge and to pursue. Thus not only does the state lose significant revenue but the masses working in the informal sector enjoy existences at best uncertain and at worst impoverished. Only when a far greater proportion of Black Africans come to enjoy employment within an expanded formal sector will their general level of prosperity increase. This situation has implications, long term, for the country's political stability.

## Land

Of all the issues on Southern Africa's socio-economic scene, that of land gives rise to the greatest emotion. This is particularly marked in the cases of South Africa and Zimbabwe, though it is a problem throughout the region. Its roots lie in the colonial era, when land allocations between Black and White were grossly disproportionate, but since independence the situation has been exacerbated by unsound indigenous governance and a degree of political inertia in addressing the problem systematically. Tenure arrangements remain to a greater or lesser extent flawed and insecure and governments have yet to decide whether they should determine their land policies on the basis of enhancing agricultural efficiency or on that of promoting a greater measure of socio-economic equality: these two desirable objectives are to a considerable extent in conflict.

Little by way of a viable land policy has yet emerged in Angola. The country was locked in civil war between independence in 1975 and the death of Jonas Savimbi in 2002 and understandably the government has seen its prime task as repairing its ravages. Some three million people had been displaced from their homes by the time hostilities closed and much extra-legal land grabbing had occurred in the course of fighting by both MPLA and UNITA political elites. The prime need now is to devise laws and create legal machinery, which will enable claims for restitution of land to be fairly adjudicated. This will not be easy, given the confusion which still exists in the country and the continuing illegal occupation of large areas of land by these miscellaneous political groupings. In these circumstances, the Luanda government is considering whether a return to customary law might be the fairest way of determining which communities have historical rights to which land and, hopefully, it will have the political will to enforce these against the illegal occupiers.

In Mozambique, progress with land policy has been rather better, though substantial problems remain. The Land Policy of 1995 and the subsequent Land Law of 1997 have attempted to reconcile Mozambique's socialist past with the demands of the current market economy. The power of central government remains very strong: only it can authorise 'land-use rights' to individuals and communities but, thereafter, these can be transferred or bequeathed to third parties, which obviously minimises government control and promotes an incipient free market in land. Both these measures of 1995 and 1997 lay emphasis on customary law in determining how these land use allocations are made and represent a genuine attempt to decentralise rural development and alleviate poverty at the same time, however difficult it may be to strike a balance. Only time will tell how successful this will be: sadly, threats to a fair land policy still remain from unauthorised land grabbing by elites (as in Angola) as well as, on occasion, from unilateral action by Maputo (in its former *dirigiste* tradition) of shifting people off land without compensation to make way for rural development projects dear to its heart.

In Namibia, little progress with land redistribution was made in the first decade of independence; since 2000, however, this has been accelerated and government intends to redistribute 9.5 million hectares by 2008, five times more than that redistributed before 2000. The government continues to vacillate between land allocation as an alleviator of poverty on the one hand and as a rural development strategy – designed to improve agricultural production – on the other. In political and electoral terms they want the former, but in terms of economic growth the latter, and this bedevils the allocation of the land, as they have not yet decided what they can realistically ask of the new stakeholders. The passing of the Commercial Land Reform Act in 1995 enabled the government to acquire large, underutilised and foreign-owned farms for resettlement and granted it first refusal on all farmland offered for sale, subject to compensation at market rates. By the end of 2002, the government had purchased 118 farms totalling some 710,000 hectares of agricultural land out of a total of some 70 million hectares in Namibia altogether. The Communal Land Reform Act of that same year provided for the redistribution of that land according to customary law but how effectively this is likely to be implemented in terms of cost remains to be seen.

It is not possible to be altogether sanguine about how fairly and effectively Namibia's land policy will be implemented over time. A balance between poverty alleviation and a realistic rural development strategy needs to be struck and customary law needs to be vigorously enforced against the political elites who have enclosed considerable communal land for their own use – so far with impunity. This is not an easy situation to address and reflects that which already pertains in Angola and Mozambique.

It is, perhaps, in Zimbabwe that the problem of 'land hunger' has in recent years become most acute. In Rhodesia as it then was, legislation was passed in the late 1920s and during the 1930s to restrict access by Africans to approximately half the land in the country (see Map C, p. 9).[9]

This situation persisted after independence in 1980, because President Robert Mugabe felt the country needed the presence of European farmers to ensure its continuing agricultural efficiency. The bargain struck was that Europeans would be left in peace, provided they played no part in Zimbabwe's politics, and so this situation continued until late in the 1990s. The only problem with this, from the African viewpoint, was that, notwithstanding independence, the masses remained in a state of socio-economic impoverishment relative to the White minority. In practical terms, little for them had changed since UDI and this gave rise to increasing resentment with the passage of time, a resentment to which Mugabe felt impelled to respond. By 1997, he had the land of the European settlers firmly in his sights.

Since then, European farmland has been taken over forcibly, and with little or no compensation to its owners, on a very considerable scale. Marauding groups of 'war veterans' and their ZANU-PF supporters have moved into areas of White farm settlement and terrorised owners from their properties. Apart from the dispossession of these White farmers, this takeover of land has had two consequences: firstly, it has gravely debilitated Zimbabwe's agricultural potential to the extent that the country now requires food aid from abroad; secondly, it has involved the eviction of some 200,000 African farm-workers and their families from their places of employment or residence, a total of approximately 1–1.5 million people. Some of these have moved away entirely, others have remained and now scratch what living they can from the farms and their peripheries, but the stability of life and of employment which they previously enjoyed under the European aegis has vanished completely. In consequence, thousands of farms and millions of acres of productive land are now lying idle and, of the land which has been reallocated, much is in the hands of government cronies who have no knowledge of farming techniques. No machinery of tutelage or support has been established by government to address this situation. The result today is one of widespread dislocation, not to say starvation, in many areas of the country. Whatever the historic ills of the unequal situation regarding possession of Zimbabwe's land, it is hard to avoid the conclusion that the summary, brutal manner in which it is being addressed by the present government is compounding the evil, in terms both of damaging the economy and of derogating from the rule of law.

In South Africa, there remains a legacy of land inequality dating from the Native Land Act of 1913 and the Group Areas Act of 1950. Today, agricultural land is overwhelmingly in the hands of Whites, 55,000 White farmers being on 75 per cent of it and 1.2 million African subsistence farmers on the remaining 25 per cent. The inequality of this situation was recognised by the incoming Government of National Unity (GNU) in 1994 and under the Renewal and Development Plan of that year various proposals were made to address it. Current policy stems from the 1997 White Paper which speaks of the problem being tackled by three means – restitution, tenure reform and redistribution.[10] Restitution relates to land lost by Africans as a result of the aforementioned discriminatory laws and is to be in the form of return of the land, alternative land or monetary compensation. 'Tenure reform' is to ensure security – for people in their properties in African communal areas and for labour tenants against unfair eviction, especially those living on White farms. 'Redistribution' simply involves the transfer of land from those with it to those without it. To its credit, the government has set its face against condoning the kind of land invasions which have occurred in Zimbabwe.

That said, progress in recent years in addressing this inequitable and emotionally charged problem has not been very great. Some 70,000 claims for restitution are currently being processed – albeit slowly – and reforms of the tenure laws have removed some of the former anachronisms and injustices. On the redistribution front, however, progress has been at a snail's pace; under the 1997 White Paper the government proposed to transfer 30 per cent of current agricultural land into new (Black) ownership by 2015. On present showing, this is unlikely: by the end of 2003, only 1.9 million hectares (or 3 per cent of South Africa's commercial farmland) had been redistributed. The principal reason for this is that the land acquisition grants to individual households (some US$2–3,000 each) are too small to enable them to purchase White farms outright; the only way they can do this is to club together to purchase land from 'willing' Whites. Thereafter, they have insufficient funds remaining to develop the farms, a situation which has served to vitiate the whole concept of redistribution. Indeed, this is perhaps the most serious problem currently facing small African farmers: lacking, as they do, the capital available to many of their White counterparts, they need to be granted access to this on reasonable credit terms. Furthermore, they need to be assured of access to rail or road and market links, to viable water supplies and to the provision of fencing, if redistribution is not to remain a largely dead letter.

This slow pace of redistribution has occasioned considerable resentment in many quarters and the White farming community is well aware of this. Most are prepared not only to cooperate on the policy of redistribution by selling unused or underutilised land to Africans but also to pass on to them their technical farming expertise, which the latter also lack. They well realise that continuing snail-pace progress on this whole issue of land distribution could otherwise open up the spectre of land invasions Zimbabwe-style.

## Trade, aid, debt and 'breaking even'

Most countries of the Third World are indebted and those of Southern Africa are no exception. More important than the actual external debt of a country is the percentage of GDP required to service it. In the case of the Republic of South Africa, that figure is approximately 20 per cent, which is regarded by potential donors of aid and investors as much too high. This, inevitably, raises the question as to how economically efficient South Africa is going to be in the long term and whether it is going to be able to meet its obligations. The demand of the international financial community is that South Africa should reduce its budgetary deficit and, hence, its indebtedness. Only then will it qualify for continuing development loans.

However sensible this demand may be on paper, there are serious practical (and political) difficulties about implementing such a programme in short order. Firstly, the country needs to expand and refurbish its basic infrastructure, which was much neglected during the late 1980s when apartheid was coming under considerable pressure from all sides. Secondly, it needs to concentrate, for the same reason, on the training and education of all manner of semi-skilled workers, notably builders and electrical and water engineers, of which there is a dire shortage. Thirdly, the great increase in criminal violence in South Africa since 1994 means that much expenditure is needed to enhance security – principally in the country's major cities.

The security issue is particularly germane. The greater the insecurity, the lower the foreign direct investment South Africa is likely to attract from the wider world. This investment it desperately needs if it is to achieve the aforementioned objectives of improving its infrastructure and training its semi-skilled personnel. It must, therefore, do everything in its power to diminish the amount of criminal violence which seems to have become endemic in South African society. This is obviously likely to involve increased expenditure in real terms on the police, probation and other security services.

This is a sine qua non for attracting foreign direct investment, but, even assuming that this security is achieved, problems for South Africa remain. There is a distinct possibility that not only South Africa but Southern Africa generally may become marginalised in terms of foreign direct investment relative to Eastern Europe, the former Soviet Union and the Maghreb. These regions loom larger in the political and economic perception of Japan, the European Union and the USA than do the states of Southern Africa which are, by comparison, remote. Put bluntly, anything going awry in these former places is likely to impact more seriously on the OECD countries than events in Southern Africa. A further problem for Southern Africa is that both its agricultural and raw material exports to the OECD are liable to quotas to prevent 'dumping' disadvantageous to farmers in the EU, Japan and the USA. Likewise protective duties are levied after a certain point on manufactured goods made from African countries' raw materials. This situation is as disadvantageous to Southern Africa as it is advantageous to the OECD, who are anxious to protect their own processing industries; for this reason, its early reversal appears unlikely. Both Swaziland and Botswana suffer in this way regarding their sugar and beef exports to the EU, which are rigorously controlled under the Common Agricultural Policy: but for these quotas, they could export substantially more. Likewise, they would earn more if they could export leather belts rather than raw leather (Zimbabwe), canned rather than refrigerated raw fish (Angola) and packeted rather than raw sugar (Swaziland). The extra foreign exchange thus earned would serve to finance the work of indigenous processing and expand the general wage economy, thereby diminishing the situation of chronic unemployment which currently exists throughout the region. The general reluctance of the OECD to lower both its tariff and nontariff barriers to goods emanating from Southern Africa is one of the main factors contributing to poverty there.

Another problem is the volatility of the export price of Southern Africa's principal commodities. Gold and diamonds will fluctuate in price, if perhaps rather less than coffee, sugar and copper. That price is, however, determined almost totally by the demand for these products in the OECD countries: in periods of boom, such as during the Korean War in the early 1950s, they will rise and, in those of recession such as pertained in the mid-1970s after the Yom Kippur War in the Middle East, they will fall. Southern Africa has no control over this situation and their economies are moreover competitive with one another in that they are all striving for their niche in the markets of the developed world. Zambia and Zaire both aspire to sell their copper to OECD countries, as do Swaziland and Mozambique their sugar. They have no scope for selling them to one another.

Finally, a brief word about the activity of multinational corporations. These evoke much criticism from local African politicians, who charge that they 'cream off the profits'. This charge is easier to explain than to refute: multinational corporations are not philanthropic concerns by nature and are ultimately responsible to their shareholders, most of whom live far beyond the borders of Southern Africa. The repatriation of profits is an inevitable part of their whole *raison d'être* and criticism on this ground alone is misplaced. The presence of multinational activity in a country does add to its economy, its development and its employment in substantial, if varying, measure. In the early 1990s, soon after independence, the De Beers diamond company came to an arrangement with the government of Namibia that each should take a 50 per cent stake in the prospecting, production and sale of diamonds from that country. Thereby, Namibia retained a substantial stake in its not inconsiderable mining industry and was not tempted either to nationalise it or to tax it out of viable commercial existence.

Rather similarly, Rio Tinto Zinc has been active in Zimbabwe for some three decades. In 1974, it set up a gold refinery plant in the Midlands some way west of Harare and also assisted with the building of three secondary schools in the area at Zhombe, Mhondoro and Nyabata, which were then very much needed. Later, in 1988–9, it helped with the development of the area around the Renco gold mine in Masvingo Province by building the Tugwane Dam to irrigate an area which had been much affected by drought and on which many farmers had settled in smallholdings with their families. Maize, sugar, groundnuts and vegetables could thereafter be grown and these not only supplied the local Renco Township but could be transported and marketed elsewhere, thereby adding to the prosperity of the whole area. Rio Tinto also trained local people in the managerial running of the dam, mainly in basic economic management and cost accounting, before withdrawing in 1994 and handing the whole venture over to the Zimbabwean government as a going concern.[11] It may be that these two ventures could serve as models which other corporations and governments might, to their mutual advantage, emulate.

In conclusion, mention must be made of the Anglo-American Corporation of South Africa. It operates not merely in South, but throughout Southern, Africa and is an organisation of immense financial and investment power. It was founded in 1917 by Ernest Oppenheimer, who came to South Africa in 1902 from the London diamond broking firm of Dunkelsbuhlers to be their representative in Kimberley and had already impressed them as a junior clerk with his shrewdness and acumen. Their confidence was not misplaced: after working for them in South Africa until 1917, he founded Anglo-American in that year in association with the American financier J.P. Morgan and with Herbert Hoover, later to be president of the United States. His initial objective was the exploitation of the goldfields on the Eastern Rand and his success with this enabled him in 1919 to assume control of the De Beers diamond mining company. His investment shrewdness and ability to gauge financial risk (he established the Anglo-American (Rhodesian) Corporation in 1929 to exploit the copper mines of what is today Zambia) led to the rocketing success of Anglo-American as a corporation and to great personal wealth. Later, its investment activities extended well beyond mining and by the mid-1970s its annual turnover accounted for over a quarter of South Africa's GDP. Whilst much of its profits are paid out to foreign shareholders, the amount of money remaining in the country and the economic activity and employment it generates are considerable. South Africa has in recent years emerged into an increasingly globalised world and Anglo-American's shares are regularly traded on the London Stock Exchange. Were anything untoward to befall Anglo-American, the consequences not only for South Africa but for Southern Africa as a region would be dire.

## The Southern African Development Community (SADC)

SADC started life in 1980 as the Southern African Development Co-ordination Conference (SADCC) but changed its name to the Southern African Development Community (SADC) in August 1992 under the Treaty of Windhoek. During its first incarnation its members were Angola, Mozambique, Tanzania, Malawi, Swaziland, Zimbabwe, Zambia, Lesotho and Botswana and its objectives were to promote the economic development of Southern Africa without having to rely significantly on the Republic of South Africa. The SADCC was the brainchild of Presidents Kaunda and Nyerere, who had between them engineered with China the building of the Tanzam Railway from the Zambian copperbelt to the Tanzanian port of Dar-es-Salaam in the late 1960s and early 1970s precisely to avoid reliance on the Southern African rail system then dominated by South Africa and the minority regime in Rhodesia: the River Zambezi represented for them the northern frontier of White power.

All this changed in the early 1990s with the demise of the apartheid regime in South Africa. In 1990, Namibia, itself independent in that year, joined the SADCC and, two years later, the signing of the Treaty of Windhoek ushered in SADC, an organisation very different from its predecessor in the sense that, with South Africa moving towards majority rule, it was no longer regarded as 'the enemy'. Following the elections of April 1994, South Africa itself signed the Windhoek Treaty and became a fully fledged member of the Community. Mauritius subsequently joined in 1995 and the Seychelles and Democratic Republic of Congo in 1998.

The Community's principal objective was to achieve the development of its members in Southern Africa through a process of regional integration. It was intended to be more than a device for promoting economic growth; mention was also made in the Treaty of establishing common political values both between and within the member states and of preserving peace throughout the region. The economic development was to be 'rounded' and 'self-sustaining' and to be achieved through the harmonisation of national politics into a single regional strategy. SADC now needs to be viewed within the context of both the global and sub-Saharan African economies. The latter produces some US$290 billion annually and, of this, SADC accounts for some 174 billion.[12] It is thus in regard to Africa an economic grouping of considerable significance but to the global economy it is minute, representing only 0.6 per cent of world GNP. The combined GNP of sub-Saharan Africa is slightly larger than Argentina's and slightly smaller than Switzerland's. If sub-Saharan Africa's 42 countries are to advance in prosperity, a much greater degree of economic integration between them is vital, as this would allow greater economies of scale and greater specialisations of production. SADC was formed in 1992 with precisely this integration in mind.

Progress on this during the first 15 years of SADC's existence has not, however, been very great. Firstly, South Africa apart, the competitive nature of the various states' economies has been mainly responsible for this. These have been too similar to integrate and to specialise in particular goods and their capacities for industrial production have remained extremely limited. What has happened in each of the countries, including South Africa, has been the expansion of the informal sector. This, though extremely important for the individual countries themselves, has little role to play in economic integration at regional level. It is not possible, for example, for car-breakers and spare-parts cannibalisation concerns, or street-trading chains, to be established at this level. Economic activity has tended to become familial and fragmented to a high degree. It has been estimated that, throughout the SADC region, between 20 and 25 per cent of the economy is to be found in the informal sector and for the economies to integrate in the medium to long term this figure must reduce.

Secondly, SADC itself is an unbalanced community. Nearly 80 per cent of its 200 million population is concentrated in the DRC and South Africa, with relatively small populations in the other member states. The wealth of the region is concentrated in the five South African Customs Union (SACU) states of Namibia, Botswana, Lesotho, Swaziland and, most notably, South Africa: these countries have between them 88 per cent of its telephones, 72 per cent of its air traffic and 62 per cent of its rail track and macadamised roads. If SADC is to integrate successfully, this infrastructural strength needs to be more widely spread around the other nine member states, as does its population.

Thirdly, SADC needs to come to trade within itself much more: most of its trade is with the developed world, only 5 per cent of it is intra-regional. Of SACU imports, only 2 per cent originate in SADC countries, whereas 11 per cent of SACU exports go to SADC – which exemplifies the strength of SACU and the relative inability of the non-SACU states to export. This is due partly to the aforementioned lack of infrastructure and partly to low scores on the human development index. In no way can SADC be likened to the EEC at its inception in 1958, whose members by that time were already sophisticated industrial states with a variety of goods to offer in trade.

Nor – fourthly – can SADC be compared with South Africa in any meaningful sense. South Africa's position within SADC is crucial to the whole community: without South Africa, the latter could not survive. Of SADC's US$174 billion of annual production, $140 billion comes from South Africa. South Africa also provides the main market for the non-primary product exports of the SADC states: were she for any reason to become unable to provide this, the consequences would be dire for the whole region, especially for the non-SACU states of Zimbabwe and Malawi. She needs thus to retain her role as 'lead goose' but not so stridently that her partners in SADC become inordinately deprived. South Africa's role in SADC is in many ways akin to that of the US in NATO: for both organisations to survive politically, these lead states must know how to 'punch below their weight'. Just as the US has to provide a safety-net for NATO, so also will South Africa have to bear the ultimate burden of ensuring Southern Africa's balanced development. A tribute must be paid to the intricate analysis of SADC carried out by Bradshaw and Ndegwa in their book, *The Uncertain Promise of Southern Africa*.

It is perhaps fair to state that much work still remains to be done before SADC can be said to have reached the 'broad and sunlit uplands' postulated in the Windhoek Treaty. The latter spoke of the importance of integrating the supply and demand sides of member states' economies. This requires, amongst other things, viable state infrastructures, low transportation costs within the region, complementary rather than competitive productions between the states and good marketing intelligence: most of these are basically not yet in place. Botswana's precious stones compete with those of Angola and South Africa and a generally poor transportational infrastructure means that transport accounts for some 40 per cent of the total value of goods sold within the region: this constitutes a serious non-tariff barrier to trade.

All the members of SADC appreciate the importance of industrialising to the maximum extent and of integrating their economies to enhance their overall prosperity, but to date have not shown enough political will to make the organisation fully credible. The SADC's 1996 trade protocol was intended to give a guiding light but so far only a third of its members have ratified it and two-thirds are required to do so before it can come into effect. This is because many states fear that they will lose out in the short term in the deals that will need to be struck and are reluctant to take a long-term view. The overriding problem is that, with the exception of South Africa and to a lesser extent Zimbabwe, their economies are too similar in their reliance on primary products for their earnings of foreign exchange and all compete frantically to retain their niches in the markets of the OECD states. They cannot, therefore, yet think 'regionally' but only nationally, and feel that any failure to do so will result in the loss of political support at home. The stagnation that has thus occurred in recent years over the implementation of the trade protocol does not bode well for SADC's future.

There is, moreover, a general apprehension by the smaller states of SADC that economic integration will tend not only to their disadvantage but to the further aggrandisement of South Africa as the organisation's 'lead goose'. Though they realise that they are inevitably dwarfed by their powerful neighbour to the south, they nevertheless resent this and do not wish to exchange a domineering South Africa under minority rule for a dominating one under majority rule. They would prefer to view South Africa as 'just another member' rather than as a hegemon. This preference, however, is rooted in rhetoric rather than reality. Just as they need to accept South Africa's pivotal position within SADC, so South Africa needs gracefully to accept the prospect of helping lame dogs over stiles and hope that, with time, the dogs will become less lame and the stiles less high.

## Health

The quality of health in Southern Africa is largely determined by the fact that a high proportion of the population is severely undernourished. In the continent generally 40 per cent of its people survive on less than a dollar per day and 52 per cent on less than two dollars per week: only 8 per cent can be described as 'comfortably off'. Africans are five times more likely to die before the age of five than any other people in the world and it has been estimated that no more than half of Africans

alive today will survive until the age of 60. For other developing continents, the figure is 70 per cent and, for industrialised countries, 90 per
cent.[13] This situation naturally calls for great concern at the political
level and for substantial rather than minimal public expenditure on
health services.

Sadly, however, this level of expenditure in no way pertains. In
recent years, all governments in Southern Africa have been compelled
to reduce rather than increase the proportion of their budgets devoted
to health care as a result of their adoption of 'structural adjustment'
policies. They have done this very much at the behest of the International Monetary Fund and the World Bank, who have impressed on
them that this is the price that they must expect to pay for continuing to
receive credit and development loans. Governments' acceptance of these
demands has resulted in substantially reduced public expenditure generally and on health care – notwithstanding the greatness of its need.
In particular, Zimbabwe's adoption of structural adjustment policies in
1991, when its allocation to health care was at a fairly high level, caused
this to decline by 35 per cent by 1994. This resulted in the abolition
of 400 nursing posts and the redundancy of some 800 health workers
throughout the service. The concomitant imposition of 'user fees' also
led to a substantial decline in the numbers of people using the services.[14] Similarly, by the end of the millennium, Tanzania found that she
could only devote US$3.20 per annum per head to health care despite
the fact that the World Bank had itself recommended that the minimum
acceptable figure should be US$12.80 per annum per head. Indeed the
demands of structural adjustment have meant that all the countries in
the region, apart from South Africa, are currently spending more on
the servicing of debt than they are on such public services as health and
education.[15] In addition, structural adjustment has involved the encouragement of privatisation with all the trimming of the workforce and
the imposition of 'user charges' for such things as anti-tuberculosis
therapy which this entails: it also involves cuts in food subsidies and the
enforced transfer of resources from domestic food production to that
of cash crops for export. These last two measures in particular strike a
body blow at those who are already in a most vulnerable economic situation. The work of Nana Poku is well worth perusing in this regard. It is
perhaps to be argued that OECD countries, as represented by the World
Bank and the International Monetary Fund, should look with greater
understanding on Southern African countries when they run budgetary
deficits rather than be eternally expecting them to 'pull themselves up
by their bootstraps', bootstraps which in fact they scarcely possess.

Of all the various maladies which afflict Southern Africa, HIV/AIDS is the most immediate and the most threatening: indeed, for the past 20 years, it has been the bane of the entire subcontinent, gathering pace as the 1980s progressed. By the early 1990s, it could no longer be ignored. At the present time, some 28 million people throughout Africa are thought to be HIV-positive or actually to have AIDS; over the last 15 years some 17 million persons have died of it. It is instructive that whilst 200,000 Africans perished in Africa's various wars in 1998, two million died of AIDS.

In Southern Africa itself, 16 per cent of Malawi's population is HIV-positive and 20 per cent of Zambia's. In South Africa, the situation is rather less bad, but 10 per cent of its population are currently estimated to be HIV-positive. One of the more distressing features of the South African scene is the vast increase in the number of pregnant women found to be HIV-positive (up from 0.7 per cent of those examined in 1990 to 22 per cent in 1998) and 200 HIV-positive children are born each day in South Africa. An extrapolation from these various figures suggests that 40–50 per cent of the adult working population is likely to be lost by the end of the present decade unless steps can be taken to roll back the disease. The collateral costs, in terms of both finance and mental anguish for patients and their families, can only be guessed at.

There are a number reasons for this sad phenomenon. One has been the incidence of civil strife in such countries as Angola and Mozambique. As experience in both Rwanda and the Democratic Republic of Congo came to show, women are particularly vulnerable to sexual violence when they have been forced to flee their homes and, in consequence, inevitably lay themselves open to the attention of marauding soldiers. When they try to cross borders they may endure similar treatment from border officials and when they enter refugee camps they are likely to come under pressure from those in charge or from other refugees. Indeed the situation in which these unfortunate women find themselves is often one in which life is nasty, brutish and short.

This, however, is not the main reason for the increase in the disease: a further and yet more important factor is the increasing mobility of Southern African society. Even in Malawi, one of the region's smaller countries, there is a much greater flow of people between town and country than there used to be and this has had a negative impact on the traditional calm and sobriety of rural life. Country women encounter passing men, such as soldiers and truck drivers, much more than once they did. These men constitute a particular source of infection and the women are not yet sufficiently knowledgeable about basic health matters and the dangers of becoming HIV-positive. This situation applies equally throughout Southern Africa.

What is particularly sad is that these rural Malawian women – and indeed women in the region generally – are often infected with the virus by their own husbands on their return from migrant labour contracts in South Africa which has traditionally run a system of migrant labour for its gold and diamond mining industries, in which men from Malawi have participated on contracts of one or two years' duration. During this period of separation from their wives and families they have few leisure outlets other than booze and casual sex. The upshot is that they frequently become infected and carry this infection back to their wives when they return home on the expiry of their contracts, thereby spreading the disease.

Likewise in South Africa, a similar situation applies. The town of Carletonville on the Rand has a working population of 85,000, the overwhelming majority migrant workers. Of these, some 65,000 are HIV-positive: when they return home, they infect their wives. A study undertaken in KwaZulu Natal in 1999 showed that 13 per cent of women whose husbands worked on contract for months on end away from home became HIV-positive, whereas amongst women whose husbands worked locally no infection was recorded.[16]

If these are the principal causes of the current pandemic, the consequences are no less serious. The disease is going to affect both the quantity and quality of the labour force in the years immediately ahead. Many will perish and be absent from work in the run-up to their decease. Children will be withdrawn from school both to help look after members of the family who are suffering and to supplement family income: those still less fortunate are likely to end up as orphans themselves. Those who care for AIDS sufferers will at intervals be absent from their work, if indeed they can work at all, and attendance at funerals will become the rule rather than the exception. Yet more devastating is the fact that the high incidence of an HIV-positive population will make other diseases such as tuberculosis (TB) more difficult to treat successfully. The 1990s saw 30 million deaths from TB worldwide: many of these would have been saved but for the damage done to their immune systems by their HIV-positivity. TB can now be cured readily and affordably in people who are basically healthy.

To achieve an improvement in this situation, three steps need to be taken. Firstly, there needs to be a change in socio-sexual attitudes on the part of males, who tend all too readily in this matter to 'equate the pleasurable with the good'. It needs to be borne in on them, by way of an intensive public enlightenment campaign, that the wages of fornication and adultery are likely to be illness and premature death, the short-term pleasurability notwithstanding.

Secondly, there needs to be yet more emphasis on the education of women, particularly rural women, about the incidence of HIV/AIDS and how the associated pressures can best be combated. Evidence has already shown that the more education women have acquired, the less early they marry and, in consequence, the fewer (and healthier) children they bear. [17] They are more able to control their lives and thereby to enhance its overall quality. A UN Report on AIDS of 1999 drew a strong correlation between high literacy rates for women and low rates of infant mortality. It is changes in attitudes and behaviour rather than the greater availability of retroviral drugs (important though these are) that will be crucial to alleviating a situation which was described by then President Bill Clinton in 1998 as a 'security threat to the whole industrialised world' and by the Commonwealth Heads of Government in 1999 as a 'global emergency'. South Africa's former president, Nelson Mandela, too, is on record as follows:

> Aids represents a tragedy of unprecedented proportions unfolding particularly in Africa but with effects across the globe. It is claiming more lives in Africa than the sum total of all wars, famines and floods and the ravages of such deadly diseases as malaria.

It is most regrettable that, since becoming president, Thabo Mbeki has downplayed the seriousness of the AIDS pandemic, denying its connection with promiscuous behaviour and not using his best endeavours to secure supplies of retroviral drugs at generally affordable prices.

Thirdly, and in conclusion, something needs to be done to ensure that the quality of nutrition in Southern Africa improves markedly. The problem is widespread: malnutrition stems partly from poverty and partly from ignorance. Many Africans, moreover, simply do not appreciate the importance of a balanced diet and kwashiorkor, caused by lack of protein, remains an all-too common complaint. Lack of fresh vegetables and deficiencies of vitamin A also have deleterious effects and infant children who have insufficient of these nutrients run the serious risk of becoming prematurely blind, but, more generally, people who are not properly nourished become much more susceptible to the HIV/AIDS virus than those who are. Massive education programmes are required to bring home to people the importance of balanced nutrition, but the structural adjustment programmes aforementioned may well lead to the deletion, on financial grounds, of this kind of endeavour. More resources, too, need to be devoted to food production for domestic consumption rather than to cash crops for export, even if this has a negative effect, pro tem, on the balance of payments. Clearly, a balance over this sensitive matter will have to be struck, but, equally, it is evident that a helter-skelter rush to satisfy the demands of the market and of sound macro-economics will do little to alleviate a problem which is eating away at the very body of Southern Africa and which will, in time, come to affect the wider world.

## The status of women

Even though Southern Africa may have achieved a revolution during the past quarter of a century, the same cannot be said about the status of women. In numerous walks of life, they remain to a greater or lesser extent disadvantaged and, when one remembers that 52 per cent of the region's population is female, this detracts substantially from its overall development. At grassroots level, women work 'in the shadows' much more than men: husbands are often absent on migrant labour contracts and the burden of feeding the family and managing the home falls disproportionately on their wives. Women's work is often unrecorded and unsung, whereas men's shows up much more clearly at the workplace and in official labour statistics. Men, when they are at home, are usually reluctant to help with domestic work, a phenomenon which, whilst not entirely unknown in Europe, tends to be strongly characteristic of African male culture. This adds notably to the burden already borne by women.

There is thus a culture of 'patriarchy' in Southern Africa, which is not going to be easy to overcome. Former President Nelson Mandela recognised this at the opening of South Africa's first multiracial parliament in May 1994 when he affirmed that the objectives of the Renewal and Development Plan could only be realised if the condition of South African women changed greatly for the better.[18] He called for their 'empowerment', for them to be put on a par with men in all aspects of life. His first White Paper in the RCD published just over a year later in June 1995 spoke of removing gender discrimination in public works employment, loosening credit constraints on women without substantial collateral and improving their access to child care. Events since have disappointed the promise of that declaration. The ANC government, now re-entrenched with a new mandate, is going to have to be much more proactive on the legislative front, in other words more 'top down' in its approach, if the current continuing anachronisms are going to be dismantled.

What are the principal anachronisms? Firstly, violence against women. The law is going to have to be amended to discourage this in both public and private places. Women are, sadly, unsafe in the region generally:

South Africa's rape statistics are among the highest in the world. Secondly, there is a tradition whereby women's assets, and land especially, tend to be held not in their own name but in that of a close male relative. This is particularly the case in rural areas, where customary law applies more rigidly, despite the fact that this conflicts with the gender discrimination clauses of the 1996 Constitution. It is important for both the personal dignity of women and their underlying economic security that they should be able to hold assets and land in their own name, since this would increase their entitlement to credit on terms similar to men. Here again, a change in the law is long overdue. Thirdly, women tend to be discriminated against in the labour market because of their fecundity, whether or not they have children actually in tow. Very nearly half of all the pregnancies in South Africa occur to girls still in their teens, thus they cannot access job vacancies with the same ease as men and for this reason, as already stated, they tend to work in the shadows and do not show up in the employment statistics. Discrimination of this kind needs to be swept away and this can only be achieved by appropriate legislation.

At the lowest end of the scale, in farming in the former Bantustans, much of the physical labour is actually carried out by women, often in the most arduous conditions, and the law in these rural areas means that, though they may have access to the land, they have no rights to either its ownership or its produce. They are thus in a position similar to that of medieval serfs. The Commission of Gender Equality, created under the 1996 Constitution, is well aware of this problem and has placed land reform at the head of its agenda with the intention of improving both access and security of tenure for rural women.[19] However, little progress has been made to date and the commission has itself been much criticised in recent years for inefficiency, inertia and financial laxity.

Notwithstanding Nelson Mandela's clarion call of May 1994, the present outlook for an improvement in women's rights remains distinctly parlous. Several things need to happen if this is to change. First, a strong and well-organised women's movement for the enhancement of their rights and opportunities needs to be established on a pan-Southern African basis: nothing of that kind currently exists. Second, mainstream organisations within South and Southern African civil society, like the professions and universities, need to concern themselves with the immediacy of the problem much more than heretofore by doing their utmost to create an awareness of the role that women can play in numerous spheres of public life and generally maximising employment outlets for them. Third, the SADC Gender Forum can reinforce this same message at governmental level, thereby diluting the male conservatism which exists in that quarter too. Fourth, and perhaps most important of all, the attitude of the average Southern African male towards his female counterpart needs to change. He needs to come to appreciate that women do not exist just for his comfort and convenience, that they have a role to play in both society and the workplace every bit as valid as his and the right to live their lives free of violence and sexual threat both in public and private places. In the long term, this can only come about through a programme of socialisation and education, which may include counselling and group therapy but which will need to be supported as necessary – and, hopefully, not too frequently – by the sanction of the criminal law.

# 2 The political dimension

## South Africa before 1948

The whole of Africa, but particularly its most southerly part, has been profoundly affected by its contact with Europe, The earliest European explorers were the Portuguese under Henry the Navigator, who rounded its shores at Senegal in 1460 and made settlements at various points on the West African coast in the years which followed. Lagos, once the capital of Nigeria, was founded in 1475 and bears the name of a Portuguese town in the Algarve, which still exists today. The Portuguese were concerned to engage in trade in gold, ivory and other commodities and, with the passage of time, a substantial trans-Saharan trade built up between Portugal and the various kingdoms of West Africa. Rather later, in 1485, the Portuguese founded settlements in Angola and, later still, in 1550, in Mozambique. They were not, at this juncture, at all interested in the acquisition of African territory in the interior, their settlements being confined to coastal areas.

Only in the second half of the seventeenth century did this situation begin to change. The Dutch East India Company sent one of its leading entrepreneurs, Jan van Riebeeck, to the Cape in 1652 with orders to establish a rest and refuelling station for the company's ships en route to the Dutch East Indies. At this time, the company's commercial activity was being gravely affected by outbreaks of scurvy amongst its ships' crews, which had resulted in much loss of life. To rectify this, the company sent Van Riebeeck to the other end of Africa to organise a settlement where the ships and their crews could both rest and be resupplied with stocks of fresh fruit and vegetables for the long journey across the Indian Ocean. With the establishment of this settlement, the toll taken of the merchantmen by scurvy rapidly diminished and, by the end of the seventeenth century, there was a substantial Dutch population of peasant farmers in and around Cape Town, which had grown as a result of Dutch East India Company policy. Slowly but surely these farmers moved into the interior of Cape Province, displacing and dominating the indigenous peoples, the San and Hottentots, as they did so. For over a century after 1700 this process continued, the Dutch population moving ever eastwards and coming, in consequence, into confrontation with the Black tribes of the interior who were themselves moving in a south-westerly direction in search of land for grazing their cattle.

The pattern of society established by the Dutch, over seven generations after 1652, had a peculiarity of its own. It was inherently hierarchical, based strictly on a master–servant relationship and a culture of order and command. Barter was common and money wages unusual and the Africans were thus very much tied to the White owner of the land on which they happened to find themselves. But, more significant even than this, the political ideas of eighteenth-century Europe, the Enlightenment, the doctrine of the Rights of Man and the ideals of the French Revolution had all passed these Dutch by, marooned as they were at the other end of the African continent. As a result of slow communications and great distances, they found themselves at the beginning of the nineteenth century trapped in a time-warp, with little appreciation of how much the world had changed since their forebears' departure from Europe in 1652.

Superimposed on this was a rigid adherence to the Protestant religion as interpreted by John Calvin. Man was essentially sinful and ignorant and the only way he could redeem himself was through constant work and prayer. If this was true for the Dutch, how much more was it true for the Black tribes over which they presided? Thus a belief grew up amongst the Dutch that they had a mission bequeathed to them by God to govern this land and the benighted Black people who dwelt there and, through wise and divinely inspired governance, bring them, however gradually, to enlightenment and salvation. This set of values made their administration paternalistic and inflexible to a degree but constituted the bedrock of Dutch political belief, or 'Afrikanerdom' as it later came to be called. The resident Dutch had organised themselves by the early nineteenth century into the Afrikaner Volk, the ideals of which imposed obligations on the whole Dutch community which few were bold enough to disregard.

The Dutch were joined by the British early in the nineteenth century – particularly after the end of the Napoleonic Wars. The British came with the active encouragement of their own government, itself anxious to encourage this emigration because of the economic depression which had set in after 1815: it wanted fewer mouths to feed and fewer unemployed. The British arrived at the Cape with a culture and outlook markedly different from that of the resident Dutch; though both were White and Christian, the similarity ended there. The British regarded the Dutch as technologically and educationally backward and lacking in respect for due process of law. Whilst themselves no liberals, they disapproved of the master–servant relationship (including a reluctance to pay money wages) on which the whole Dutch policy at the Cape depended. The Dutch saw the new arrivals as arrogant and meddlesome busybodies and the successful interference of the latter in the Dutch way of life after 1815 was the cause of the Great Trek of the mid-1830s. Many of the Dutch community loaded themselves, their families and their possessions onto ox-wagons and trekked out of Cape Province. They came, firstly, into Natal in 1836 and, in 1842, into the Transvaal and Orange Free State where, for a time, they were able to pursue their own way of life free of British interference.

The history of nineteenth-century Southern Africa is dominated as much by conflict between Boer (i.e. Dutch) and Briton as between Black and White, if not more so. Certainly, the Boers were not for long allowed to go about their business in their newly established republics. The discovery of diamonds and gold in the 1860s and 1880s rekindled British interest and involvement as well as provoking a massive influx of prospectors from overseas; two wars ensued between the British and the two Boer republics, which culminated in 1902 in the defeat of the latter and their unwilling incorporation into the British Empire. The next four years witnessed a determined attempt by the British to extirpate both the Boer culture and the Boer language, Afrikaans, from the newly unified South Africa. Although this policy was abandoned in 1906, following the election of the Liberal government in the United Kingdom, that same government, in its anxiety to reconcile Boer and Briton and to escape, thereby, the high degree of opprobrium from her European neighbours which the 1899–1902 conflict had caused to be laid at Britain's door, committed itself to a policy which was to have even graver consequences. It permitted South Africa independence as a dominion within the British Commonwealth but with a franchise which, except in Cape Province, was confined to Whites.

This policy, formalised in the South Africa Act of 1909, was fatal for the non-White peoples of South Africa, for it effectively deprived them of having any say in their own destiny; it left the question as to whether the franchise would one day be granted to them in the hands of the newly installed White government. To the extent that the issue was considered by the British parliament at all, it was generally assumed that, with the general advance over the decades of the non-Whites, the White government would gradually extend the franchise to them. This

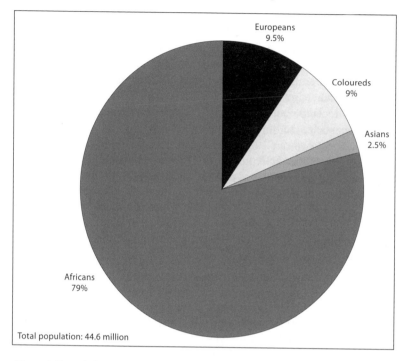

*Figure 1* Population of South Africa (source: October 2001 Census).

assumption proved naïve, for no such extension was ever granted (see Figure 1).

Why, it may be asked, did the Liberal government sanction a policy at once so racist, myopic and unprogressive? Firstly, it wanted to be rid of the South African 'problem' for political and diplomatic reasons of its own. Secondly, it wanted to reconcile the two mutually antagonistic White communities and realised that, to achieve this, it could not grant the vote to the mass of the Black population, since this would infuriate the Boers. Thirdly, it genuinely believed that the non-Whites in general, and the Blacks in particular, were too unsophisticated to be politically conscious. These three factors all conspired to persuade the Liberal government to enact the legislation in the way it did.

Thus, in 1909, the dragon's teeth were sown. To secure British–Boer reconciliation, political power passed to the White minority. The price of this was paid by the non-White majority consisting of the Cape Coloureds, the Asians and the Africans. The South Africa Act made them helots in their own country, a helotry which was to endure for some eight decades and which became more intense with the passage of time. The legislation passed during those early years, the Native Land Act of 1913, the Mines and Works Amendment Act of 1926 and many others, concerned mainly the social and economic dimensions of public life, whereby the 'poor' and educationally unqualified Whites, mainly of Boer stock, were artificially protected from the full rigour of competition in the market by racial labour quotas – a policy known as 'civilised labour'.[1] In the political field, the Representation of Natives Act 1936 deprived Africans in Cape Province of the franchise, the one area of the country where Africans possessing the required income and educational qualifications had been allowed to vote since 1853. These laws, whilst repressive, were far less comprehensive in their scope than they later became. The victory of the National Party in the 1948 general election ushered in a new era which was to last for over 40 years, the era of 'apartheid'. By this victory the Boers, after some 150 years of struggle against both Blacks and the British, came finally into their own.

## South Africa 1948–74

For much of the 1910–48 period, South African politics had been dominated by the United Party of Field Marshal J.C. Smuts. Smuts, though himself a Boer, conceived partnership between the two White communities to be essential to South Africa's economic and political future; in this sense, he represented the hopes and aspirations on which independence had been granted by the British in 1910. During the First World War, as a member of the Imperial War Cabinet, he had openly collaborated with the British. This collaboration was resented by many Boers and roundly condemned by the National Party, reconstituted under the leadership of D.F. Malan in 1934. Not for a moment did the latter see South Africa's future in terms of British–Boer partnership; what mattered for him was the institutionalisation of Boer supremacy and the ideals of the Afrikaner 'Volk'. Control of South Africa should revert to those who first colonised it in the 1650s and the role of the British should be that of adjutant to the Boer generals. Even though they might be equal in social terms and indeed superior in educational and professional terms, they would never be the political and governmental equals of the Afrikaners. The progress made by the National Party even before the Second World War is evinced by the fact that the South African Parliament sanctioned the Union's participation in that war by only the narrowest of majorities, the Nationalists voting solidly for South Africa's neutrality.

With the war over, the Nationalists were able to appeal successfully for a radical mandate in the general election of 1948. They argued that Smuts' United Party had become too obligated to business, financial and mining interests and in the process had permitted Blacks to flood into the main industrial and urban areas, thereby constituting a serious economic and social challenge to the White community. They played on White fears of the *swart gevaar* ('Black peril') and this factor was not fully appreciated – and hence not well rebutted – by Smuts and the United Party, who believed, rather complacently, that the government's record during the war and after would stand them in good electoral stead. This did not happen and the Nationalists under Malan took power; their victory constituted a watershed in the history of South Africa.

It constituted a watershed in that discrimination between the different racial groups within South Africa became the legal and constitutional norm. There had been discrimination between the races in South Africa from very early times, the first Pass Laws, for example, dating from 1806 and the more recent land and industrial legislation aforementioned had been oppressive in their effects. After 1948, however, it became pervasive and ubiquitous. The Afrikaners (as the Boers had by now become known) argued that the various races of South Africa were so inherently different from one another both in nature and in terms of human development potential that there was no possibility of any unity or even collaboration between them in the task of building the South African polity – except at the workplace. The only feasible way forward was for the several races – Whites, Coloureds, Asians and Africans – to develop separately in their own way and at their own pace, the whole process being stage-managed by the White community with the Afrikaners in the first and the British in the second league. This doctrine, which came to be known as 'apartheid',[2] was to dominate the politics of South Africa for over four decades.

Nor was the legislation inaugurating this new era slow in coming to the statute book. Between 1948 and 1953, a series of laws were passed to enforce differentiation between the races in a variety of ways. Of these, the Population Registration Act of 1950 was perhaps the most noteworthy: this provided that everyone should be racially classified at birth as European, Coloured, Asian or African and constituted the cornerstone of the whole apartheid system. Firstly, it enabled the authorities to reorganise the whole society along racial lines and, secondly, it determined the kind of life an individual, by virtue of his classification, would live in that society. The Group Areas Act of 1950 gave to the minister of native affairs the powers to designate which land be occupied by which race and thereby to minimise their commingling. This reclassifying of land often resulted, in subsequent years, in breaking up established communities in a harsh and arbitrary manner. In 1949 and 1950, the Mixed Marriages and Immorality Acts respectively prohibited marriage and sexual relations between White and non-White. In 1953, the Separate Amenities Act determined that separate facilities for the races should be provided for all areas of human activity – from public lavatories to bathing beaches – and there was no stipulation that the facilities should be of equal quality. It was these five pieces of legislation that constituted the core of the whole apartheid system and essentially put a stranglehold on non-White social and economic activity. What was more, the whole system was underpinned by a degree of public surveillance and control that made it difficult for anyone to challenge or defy the status quo. The Suppression of Communism Act of 1951, the General Law Amendment Act of 1963 and the Terrorism Act of 1968 all gave the authorities substantial powers over freedom of the person, which only the brave or the foolhardy were willing to flout. These laws, by virtue of their loose and discretionary phraseology, enabled ministers, officials and policemen to assume and wield powers which would have been quite unacceptable in an American or West European judicial context.[3] The majority of White South Africans accepted this situation as part of the natural order of things; the liberal minority winced and averted its gaze and a few brave souls in public life spoke out against it, experiencing often opprobrium and sometimes indeed repression as a result. Helen Suzman had to endure much social ostracism from her parliamentary counterparts for expressing her liberal views,[4] and Donald Woods was amongst those who experienced 'house arrest' for expressing similar sentiments in his capacity as a journalist.

For 25 years after 1948, the apartheid regime proceeded, under Nationalist leadership, to consolidate itself. In parliament, with the striking exceptions of Mrs Suzman's Progressive Party and Alan Paton's Liberal Party, it faced little challenge. The official opposition, the United Party, led by de Villiers Graaf, criticised the practice rather than the principle of apartheid and accepted the fruits of this inherently unequal system. The African National Congress, founded in 1912 to campaign for the political rights of the Black population, had long sought dialogue with Pretoria on this issue, but its requests had either been ignored or refused. Its approach had always been pacific and negotiatory, but by 1962 the ANC Executive Committee (of which Nelson Mandela was a leading member) called for the violent overthrow of the South African state, arguing that Pretoria's constant refusal to parley left them with no alternative. For this, Mandela and his confederates on the Executive Committee were charged with high treason and sentenced at the Rivonia Trials to terms of life imprisonment. This, coupled with the legal banning of the ANC, gave that organisation a much higher profile both within South Africa and internationally. Mandela's arrest and subsequent trial and conviction for treason in 1964 removed from the political scene someone who could have spoken for the African masses. So apartheid continued through the 1960s into the 1970s alive and well and White supremacy in South Africa was not seriously threatened. Only with the overthrow of Portuguese colonial power in Angola and Mozambique, following the military coup d'état in Lisbon in April 1974, did this situation begin to change.

## Rhodesia and Portuguese Africa before 1974

Rhodesia was originally founded from South Africa by the British South Africa Company (BSAC) under the leadership of Cecil Rhodes, who dreamed of finding a 'second Rand' in the territory then known as Zambezia. Whilst little gold was found, members of Rhodes' 'settler column' stayed and farmed the territory, notwithstanding the opposition of the Matabele king, Lobengula. Once his power had been neutralised in 1890, the Union Jack was raised in Salisbury; thereafter, the territory was renamed 'Rhodesia' and ruled from Cape Town as an outpost of Rhodes' commercial empire. After Rhodes' death in 1902, the BSAC's 'de facto' control of Rhodesia weakened and it was eventually, in 1923, sold to the British government for the sum of £4 million in cash.

The British then proceeded, given the unusually high incidence of Whites in the territory, to grant it special status as a 'self-governing colony'. This meant that it would control its own affairs with the exception of foreign policy and the colonial constitution, which were retained by London. Specifically, it meant that the 30,000 White settlers could control its defence budget and its own armed forces. The British took the view that the settler population, predominantly of British stock, was quite capable of running its own administration and that formal Colonial Office control was an expensive and unnecessary luxury. London approved a constitutional arrangement, whereby, in order to vote, citizens were expected to have £100 per annum income and to show a certain degree of educational prowess; this excluded, implicitly but not explicitly, the overwhelming majority of the Black population, who did not possess the requisite qualifications.

This arrangement lasted three decades until the establishment of the Central African Federation in 1953. It was then amended to give the citizenry votes on a dual roll, 'A' or 'B'. The former and politically more powerful roll commanded 50 of the parliament's 65 seats and the qualifications to vote on it were set at £720 per annum and two years' secondary education: most Europeans but very few Africans were eligible for this roll. For the 'B' roll, the qualifications were £120 per annum and completion of a course of primary education, but this roll only commanded 15 of the parliament's 65 seats.[5] Most of the Africans with a vote were eligible only for the 'B' roll rather than the politically significant 'A' roll; most, however, had no votes at all. Patrick Keatley's *The Politics of Partnership*, though written some four decades ago, remains a most authoritative – and readable – account of this whole period.

This pattern of White supremacy was rather more subtle than that of South Africa. There were, of course, discriminatory laws relating to land apportionment and urban influx: Salisbury, for example, became a White city as early as 1929. Apartheid, however, never formed part of Rhodesia's legal system as it came to do in South Africa after 1948, nor was anyone ever barred from the franchise purely on grounds of colour. White governments could argue, with at any rate some degree of plausibility, that it was up to the Africans, by dint of hard work and education, to gain the requisite qualifications for the franchise, as indeed the Whites had had to do. It was, however, much easier for the Whites to achieve these, given the extent to which the state education budget was weighted in their favour. Virtually all of them had the vote, most on the 'A', though some, those with rather minimal education and income, on the 'B' roll. This pattern of White domination lasted, largely unchallenged, from the 1920s to the 1950s, by which time Africans' resentment at their lot was becoming increasingly clear. This came to be appreciated in Commonwealth circles and, through a process of diplomatic attrition, the British government became more sympathetic. When the Central African Federation of 1953, consisting then of the three territories of Nyasaland, Northern Rhodesia and Southern Rhodesia, was dissolved by Britain 10 years later, the two northern colonies, Nyasaland and Northern Rhodesia, were promised independence: not so Southern Rhodesia on the ground that it did not practise genuine majority rule and showed little sign of moving in that direction. Southern Rhodesia, thus denied independence, reverted to its original status as a self-governing colony and to its original name, 'Rhodesia', whilst Nyasaland and Northern Rhodesia gained independence as Malawi and Zambia respectively in 1964.

This turn of events greatly disconcerted the Rhodesian government, which in April 1964 came to be headed by Ian Smith of the Rhodesian Front. Smith and his cabinet colleagues felt that, unless decisive action were taken, the rising tide of African nationalism before which the British government had bowed in Malawi and Zambia would soon engulf Rhodesia. This would mean the end of 'Christianity and civilised standards'.

An even stronger, but unarticulated, concern was that it would also mean the end of White supremacy and with it the cosseted life style which the vast majority of Europeans enjoyed. This was maintained on a foundation of great economic inequality. Disparate pay scales were operative for Black and White engaged on the same work and, as already mentioned, budgetary allocations between the races were grossly disproportionate. The various Land Apportionment Acts passed since 1931 prevented Africans from buying land in the more fertile areas of the country which were also better served by road and rail links (see Map C, p. 9).

The Smith government feared, especially after the accession of a Labour administration in London in October 1964, that all this would be threatened. Smith wanted independence, naturally, but only on terms which would leave the Whites in charge. 'NIBMAR' (no independence before majority African rule), upon which the new London government was insisting, was anathema to Smith and his colleagues, who realised that London had the legal and constitutional power to force these changes on them. To avert this possibility, Smith crossed the Rubicon on 11 November 1965, declaring that henceforth Rhodesia was to be an independent state and in no way subject to the British Crown. Smith felt in a strong position for several reasons: first, he as prime minister controlled Rhodesia's armed forces as a result of the 1923 settlement; second, Rhodesia, being a landlocked country about 350 miles from the coast, was difficult of military access; and, third, Harold Wilson, the new British prime minister, had in October 1965, at an interview at Salisbury Airport, ruled out the use of force in dealing with the problem of 'a unilateral declaration of independence'.

UDI, as it thereafter came to be known, had the effect of taking some five million Africans out of the protection of the British government and placing them willy-nilly under the control of 220,000 Whites. It was the latter, overwhelmingly, who had the franchise and formed the government, as already described. Though the newly independent Rhodesia did not secure the recognition of any other country, not even of South Africa or Portugal, and though UDI was combated by economic sanctions in 1966 mounted at the behest of the UN Security Council, Smith was able to maintain his illegal regime until the end of the 1970s. Wilson's assertion early in 1966, that economic sanctions would bring the Smith regime to its knees in 'weeks rather than months', did not stand the test of time. Moreover, in the 14 years that UDI was maintained, an official state of emergency persisted under which those of liberal persuasion, both White and Black, suffered house arrest, imprisonment and worse without ever being brought to court on a formal charge.[6] To a great extent, the responsibility for this unhappy situation must be laid at Britain's door: had the Wilson government been less irresolute in dealing with UDI when it occurred, its grim consequences, notably the spilling of much blood, both Black and White, might have been avoided.

The Portuguese were the first Europeans to colonise Africa and the last to leave it. Their sojourn in their three colonies of Guinea, Angola and Mozambique lasted for some 500 years. Their colonial philosophy differed from that of their European counterparts in a number of important respects.[7]

Firstly, they saw themselves as holding their power in permanent trust for the benefit of the people they colonised. Their colonisation was a beneficent force designed to uplift the people in their charge from a state of savagery. For the Portuguese, there was no such thing as African culture: only when the African had gained *assimilado* status – in other words, could speak and write Portuguese – and achieved a certain educational prowess could he be regarded as civilised. For those falling short of this goal, there was the 'ennobling virtue of work'; non-assimilated Africans were enjoined to work on contract for six months every year for a European employer.

Secondly, discrimination on the ground of race was unknown in Portuguese Africa. The early Portuguese settlers had left their homeland without their wives and there had been much cohabitation with the indigenous women: the result was the growth over several centuries of a mulatto population. The Portuguese came to consider that the latter could mix freely with them provided they were assimilated. Apartheid, therefore, was never practised in the Portuguese territories: assimilated Africans enjoyed the same rights, few though these were, as the Portuguese residents. In practice, however, only a tiny minority of Africans succeeded in gaining this status, illiteracy amongst the general African population being of the order of 99.6 per cent. The educated few could eat in the best restaurants of Lourenço Marques, provided, of course, that they could pay the bill, a situation which would never have been allowed in South Africa or indeed in White Rhodesia. Whereas in the two latter countries discrimination was a legal matter, in Portuguese Africa it was an economic and social one. In practice, there was discrimination, because, as in Rhodesia, the genuine opportunities for African advancement were few and far between.

Thirdly, there was no such thing in Mozambique, Angola or Guinea as 'settler power'. This had been a problem for the British in Kenya and, of course, Rhodesia, whereas in Portuguese Africa power resided always with a colonial governor appointed on contract by Lisbon, who ruled on its behalf without being obligated to take into account the opinion of either the White or Black residents of the particular colonial territory. They had no votes any more indeed than had the nationals of metropolitan Portugal. It was a system paternalistic in the extreme and it was scarcely surprising if the colonial regime was only in the scantiest of touch with public opinion. Given the gulf between Black and White in socio-economic terms, it was uncertain how far a coherent public opinion actually existed.

Finally, there was the concept of imperial mystique. If Portugal's mission in Africa were God-given, this made her much more than just a small European state: it put her on a par with the great and the good. Salazar speaking about Portugal's empire in 1933 said this: 'Africa is for us a justification and *raison d'être* as a great power: without it, we would be a small nation. With it, we are a great country.'[8]

For the rest of his days, Salazar clung fast to the mysticism surrounding Portugal's empire and was quite uncompromising in his belief that it should remain in perpetuity and be a source of benefit to its inhabitants. His policy was not amenable to criticism, either by those in the territories or outside them, and was to be defended to the death against the atavistic forces of African nationalism. Salazar deliberately chose to disregard the 'wind of change' of which Harold Macmillan had spoken so eloquently in the South African Parliament in February 1960 with these words:

> A wind of change is blowing through this continent and, whether we like it or not, the growth of African political consciousness is a fact and we must all accept it as a fact. Our national policies must take account of it.

This sage admonition was heeded neither by the South African government (to whom it was addressed) nor by the Salazar administration in Lisbon. Salazar was confident that he could readily outface the raggle-taggle, uncoordinated and underequipped forces of the various African nationalist groupings, but in the early 1960s liberation wars erupted in Mozambique, Portuguese Guinea and Angola. For some years, Salazar was successful, but these were wars of attrition and their cost was constantly growing. By the early 1970s Lisbon was devoting something in excess of 40 per cent of its total budget to maintaining its imperial position in Africa. The government was prepared to sustain this financial burden – but failed to appreciate that the Army was no longer willing to bear the public humiliation which its inability to contain the nationalist fighters had engendered among the population generally. Since 1961, the prestige of the armed forces had been declining: in NATO they had played little part. Conscript soldiers returning from Africa on leave were laughed at in the streets and so were their officers. With dramatic swiftness, in the last week of April 1974, the Caetano government was overthrown by the army and, almost immediately, the new military leader, General Spinola, announced his government's intention to withdraw totally and rapidly from its African empire. This withdrawal, complete by November 1975, was to have momentous consequences for the whole of Southern Africa.

### The repercussions of Portuguese imperial withdrawal 1974–8

Portugal's withdrawal from Angola and Mozambique broke the phalanx of territories behind which the Whites had been able to preserve their hegemony. In Rhodesia, Smith's illegal regime was no longer cocooned along its eastern frontier by a friendly colonial power. On the contrary, the new government of Mozambique, headed by Samora Machel, extended a warm welcome to the ZANU nationalist forces led by Robert Mugabe. On the other side of the continent, the Portuguese departure precipitated a civil war in Angola between three distinct nationalist movements and into this conflict, at an early stage, Cuba and the Soviet Union came to be drawn – at the express invitation of one of the movements, the Marxist-Leninist-orientated MPLA under the leadership of Agostino Neto. This created a strategic uncertainty for South Africa of a kind it had not previously had to face (see Map F).

For the Smith regime, the breaking of the cocoon transformed the security situation in Rhodesia. Prior to 1974, Smith and his cabinet had been able to outface the guerrilla armies of ZAPU and ZANU based in Zambia and Mozambique respectively. The country had been under military challenge, certainly, but in no way under direct military threat. Now the whole of Rhodesia's eastern frontier with Mozambique became vulnerable to attack from ZANU under the leadership of Robert Mugabe: rather less seriously, attacks by ZAPU from Zambia increased under the auspices of Joshua Nkomo. To combat this situation, the Smith government called up all adult males under the age of 45 to serve for three to four months at a time in the bush war against these guerrilla armies. This service did not prove popular and many young – and not so young – White Rhodesians voted with their feet and emigrated to South Africa: this resulted in a drain on the military muscle Smith had been counting on to preserve his unconstitutional regime. P. Moorcraft has made a detailed and perceptive analysis of this scenario (as well as those of Angola, Mozambique and Namibia) in his book *African Nemesis*.[9]

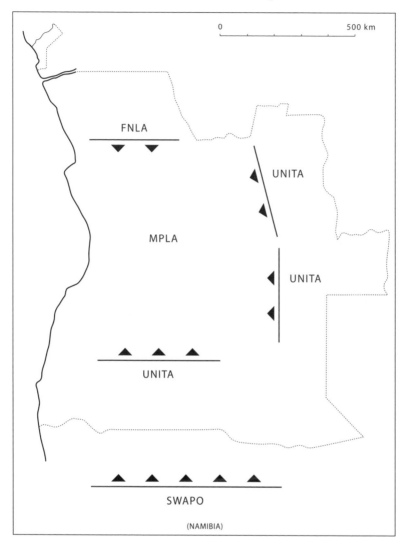

*Map F*  The civil war in Angola, 1976–84.

As the 1970s advanced, so did the appeal of African nationalism and guerrilla military power. Before the decade was up, Smith came to realise that he could no longer outface both this politico-military challenge and the strains which international economic sanctions were imposing on the country. Nor could he take South African support for granted, as he had been able to do up to 1974, for the republic was likewise experiencing the chill blasts of Southern Africa's 'wind of change'. Both P.W. Botha and, more especially, J.B. Vorster in the period 1974–9 urged Smith to come to an accommodation with his African antagonists in short order and secure what terms he could for the White settler community. Neither of these premiers relished their country being dragged, on Rhodesian coat tails, into the heat of the Southern African political arena. It was the combination of these various pressures plus an antipathetic personal relationship between him and Vorster which constrained Smith, firstly, to seek an 'internal settlement' with the 'moderate' Black African leadership of Abel Muzorewa, Ndabaningi Sithole and Chief Chirau in the United African National Council and secondly, when this failed to gain either internal acceptability or international recognition from any quarter, to negotiate with London an end to UDI and transition to majority rule by way of free elections. In April 1980, the Union Jack, first raised in Salisbury 90 years before, came down for the last time in Harare, the newly named capital of Zimbabwe.

For South Africa, the effects of the collapse of Portuguese colonial power in Angola and Mozambique were no less serious than for Rhodesia. The forces of African nationalism now confronted South Africa directly on the north-eastern frontier of the Transvaal and across Angola's Cunene River against South West Africa. More seriously for South Africa, Portugal's precipitate withdrawal from Angola had occasioned a situation of political confusion, in which none of the three Angolan nationalist movements predominated – with the result that civil war broke out in that country even before the end of 1974. Early in 1975, the USSR intervened, along with Cuba, to provide military assistance to the Popular Movement for the Liberation of Angola (MPLA), with which it had for long had close ideological links, against the two non-Marxist movements, the FNLA (the National Front for the Liberation of Angola) and UNITA (the National Union for the Total Independence of Angola), which were dominant in the northern and southern parts of the country respectively (see Map F, p. 51). To prevent the triumph of the MPLA in this war, which was perceived as a direct strategic threat to its position in South West Africa, South Africa became directly involved helping UNITA and the FNLA against the MPLA and their Soviet and Cuban backers.

South Africa could not, however, prevail in this endeavour. So massive was the help given to the MPLA by its two supporters that Pretoria decided after a few months to withdraw in good order south across the Cunene River and consolidate the South African position in Northern Ovamboland. Whilst South Africa had in no way sustained a military defeat, it was clear to all concerned that it had sustained a severe psychological one. It had avoided becoming entangled in a situation analogous to US involvement in Vietnam but at the price of leaving 'the forces of international communism' in control immediately to its north. South Africa was at last seen to be no longer politically and militarily invincible and this was reflected by the outbreak of riots in Soweto in June 1976, which, during the next few months, spread to townships in other parts of South Africa. These riots were triggered by Pretoria's insistence that, in the upper reaches of the African primary school system, Afrikaans (which most children of that age could not speak) should be used as the teaching medium. However, they would probably not have reached the level of intensity they did if Africans, generally, had not had the impression that Pretoria was vulnerable over the issue of its involvement in the Angolan civil war. That the riots were brutally suppressed by the South African authorities does not detract from this fact. Quite how things would have developed thereafter had J.B. Vorster remained prime minister is uncertain, but following the latter's implication in the 'Muldergate affair' he resigned and was succeeded in 1978 by P.W. Botha.

## South Africa 1978–94

Botha was much more pragmatic than Vorster in his whole approach to policy. The latter had, before becoming prime minister, been minister of justice and retained a certain mind-set in his attitude to non-Whites. Botha had been Vorster's defence minister, which kept him remote from the domestic political scene but gave him time to reflect upon it. He had come to the conclusion that the events of 1974–5 had altered the whole political configuration of Southern Africa, that apartheid was increasingly outmoded and impractical and that the Black–White confrontation witnessed at Soweto and other African townships in 1976 would neither be viable as a continuing policy domestically nor acceptable internationally. Change, in other words, would have to come, but Botha was determined that it should be on terms managed and controlled by Whites.

The early years of his premiership, therefore, witnessed a legislative programme which was radical by South African standards. Much of the apartheid legislation was modified or repealed: the repeal of the 1953 Native Labour Act in 1979, for example, gave African trade unions the right to call a strike. In 1982, Africans were again allowed to attend the country's principal universities, from which the Extension of University Education Act had banned them in 1959. Expenditure on African school education was dramatically increased in this period and, in 1985, the Mixed Marriages Act of 1949 and the Immorality Act of 1950 were both scrapped, enabling the various races of South Africa to have sexual relationships and to marry across the colour line. By all appearances, South Africa was on the way to becoming a less racist society.

In practice, however, there was little change. What these various reforms did was to make life rather less intolerable for the non-White communities: in no way did they threaten the overall structure of White supremacy or improve, in any meaningful sense, the socio-economic lot of non-Whites. By removing the most obscene features of apartheid, they sought to make the system more acceptable by taking the wind out of the sails of its most vociferous critics. Significantly, there was no change made at all to the three main pillars of apartheid legislation – the Population Registration Act of 1949, the Group Areas Act of 1950 and the Separate Amenities Act of 1953.

It is scarcely surprising in these circumstances that African political opinion – in so far as it could be consulted at all – remained unimpressed. Africans complained that they were being offered the shadow rather than the substance of reform and nowhere was this more true than in the government's Tricameral Constitution, which Botha offered to the three smallest racial groups – White, Coloured and Asian – in 1983. This new constitution, promulgated in September 1983, was to have three parliamentary chambers for legislative deliberations, representing the Coloured, Asian and European communities but not the African. There was the device of the President's Council for reconciling conflict between these three chambers and the Africans' situation was explained away by reference to the vote which all Africans had by right within their own tribal territories, more commonly referred to as Bantustans (see Map D, p. 13).

Whatever good Botha may have accomplished by his numerous legislative reforms was largely neutralised by the furore which this Tricameral Constitution stirred up. The Africans resented being denied a vote and the Coloured and Asian communities saw this as a device whereby the Whites might divide and rule; Botha's bona fides were roundly questioned. Was it not hypocritical to create such a parliamentary structure, yet to leave the largest element in the population completely unrepresented within it?

It was, above all, this exclusion of Africans from the new Tricameral Constitution which led to outbreaks of violence in the townships in September 1984 and the subsequent declaration of a state of emergency by Pretoria in July 1985. Much was expected by Africans from Botha's 'Rubicon Speech' of August 1985 which, they believed, would open the way to meaningful political reforms: many White liberals shared this expectation. In the event, Botha totally rejected both the principle of universal franchise within a unitary system and any concessions on a chamber for Africans under the Tricameral Constitution. Botha furthermore excluded any reforms whilst the rioting in the townships, which he ascribed to communist agitation, continued and sent in the police to deal with any outbreak of violence. The heavy-handed behaviour of the police only served to exacerbate matters: in successive years after 1985, the townships became increasingly disorderly, violent and ungovernable – made the more so by the refusal of large numbers of their inhabitants, at the behest of the ANC, to pay municipal rent and rates. The violence was primarily directed against the townships' Black municipal leaders, who were perceived to have been collaborating with Pretoria. Botha's response was to reinforce and prolong the state of emergency: this involved an increase in the already draconian powers of the police to arrest and detain without warrant and a similar restriction on the media from fully reporting events in the townships. Botha's unrelenting persistence with the state of emergency prompted both the USA and most member states of the EC to take economic sanctions against South African exports and some multinational companies, such as General Motors and Barclays, discontinued their investment activity in South Africa altogether. As if this were not enough, the OECD countries went into general recession in 1987, which gravely affected South Africa's economy beyond the sanctions actually imposed.

By 1988, Pretoria had very little room left for manoeuvre. The state of emergency had aroused much hostility both domestically and internationally. Botha persisted in his policy of defiance, whilst turning a deaf ear to any reservations expressed within his own cabinet. He was not the wily and flexible politician he had been a decade previously and his irascible temperament made him very difficult for his cabinet colleagues to work with: there were meetings and mutterings of his ministers behind closed doors in an attempt to address an increasingly intractable situation. Then, in January 1989, Botha sustained a stroke which caused him to retreat from politics for a couple of months, Chris Heunis temporarily replacing him. Early in February Botha announced from his sickbed his intention to give up his leadership of the NP but to retain the presidency. An election for the NP leadership was at once held and F.W. de Klerk, the education minister, came to the fore. In his initial speech at the opening of a new session of Parliament, he approved the policies of his predecessor, explaining his belief that South Africa's problems could best be resolved by an emphasis on 'group rights' and that universal suffrage was not the way forward.

Notwithstanding this, de Klerk, during the seven weeks that he was at the party's helm, adopted an increasingly pragmatic attitude to policy similar to that of Botha at the outset of his presidency. He realised that 'standing pat' on existing policy was not an option: he appreciated that the Blacks in the townships needed to be assuaged and fences mended with the OECD countries. His essential achievement at this time was to consolidate the party – and indeed the cabinet – behind the need for reform. Two questions predominated: firstly, the future place of the ANC in South Africa's body politic and, secondly, the continuing detention of Nelson Mandela. De Klerk induced an atmosphere within both cabinet and party whereby these issues could be openly discussed, which had not been the case under Botha. When the latter returned to the presidency towards the end of March 1989, he discovered a situation markedly different from that of two months previously. His cabinet colleagues were no longer prepared to be so deferential to the president or unquestioning of the presidential view. Perhaps in response to this, though not fully appreciating its strength, Botha announced early in April, some two weeks after his return, that he would not contest the presidency at the elections due in September but stand down once they had been held.

He was not, in the event, able to retain office even for this time. Relations within the government from April to August became increasingly strained, Botha finding himself frequently in disagreement and sometimes at loggerheads with his cabinet colleagues. Finally, de Klerk and 'Pik' Botha, the foreign minister, announced their plan (of which Botha had no prior knowledge) to make an official visit to Zambia to discuss their inter-state relations and very much *sotto voce* to have some contact with the ANC at Lusaka. Botha, when he heard this, was furious. He told both men that he, as head of state, had to approve all foreign visits by ministers. He ordered them to cancel the trip but the two men refused to do so and, when the matter came to cabinet, Botha found himself isolated. On 14 August, after a blazing row during which Botha said he had been stabbed in the back by his closest political colleagues, he resigned and de Klerk at once took over as acting president. In the ensuing general election, the National Party retained power, albeit with a greatly reduced majority, and there was a notable swing to the multiracial Democratic Party, which argued for a universal system of adult suffrage and pleaded that South Africans debate with one another on a basis of common heritage and irrespective of race.

The political eclipse of P.W. Botha and the rise of F.W. de Klerk, taken with the overall trend of the September 1989 elections, betokened a new era in South African politics. Apartheid, whilst not dead, was under sentence of death. De Klerk, ever the pragmatist, henceforward felt strong enough to steer the ship of state with rather than against the tide. In September and October 1989, his government permitted peaceful demonstrations to take place in various parts of the country against police brutality – and, more generally, against apartheid – something which would have been unheard-of in his predecessor's day. The police were present, certainly, but were under instruction not to intervene unless law and order was positively threatened. In October, bathing places were desegregated in most parts of the country and that month also saw the release of some dozen of the ANC leadership, most notably Walter Sisulu, but not, at that juncture, Nelson Mandela. These releases were, however, significant, given the seniority of those concerned. The ANC generals had been released; only the field marshal now remained incarcerated.

On 13 December 1989, de Klerk and Mandela met for the first time. The latter, whilst confirming his readiness to make a gesture towards peace on behalf of the ANC, held to his original and consistent refusal to renounce violence as an instrument of policy. Paradoxical though this might appear, de Klerk and his colleagues decided to take the risk of releasing Mandela without preconditions. They now appreciated that no political progress would take place if he remained detained, that he constituted a greater danger to South Africa's peace and stability detained than released. They believed, also, that the 1989 election result gave legitimacy to this bold démarche, irrespective of the castigations which it would receive from the Conservative Party opposition. On 2 February 1990, at the state opening of Parliament, de Klerk announced that his government had ordered the unconditional release from prison of Nelson Mandela and the legalisation of the African National Congress, the South African Communist Party and the Pan-African Congress. In the months which followed, all the major statutes establishing the apartheid system were repealed and, by 1991, South Africa could be said to be free of a regime which had dominated all aspects of state and society for over four decades. This is not to say that the dismantling process was easy or the resentments and fears quickly overcome during the period 1990–4, but that they were overcome to the extent they were must be attributed entirely to the political partnership between de Klerk and Mandela. The former appreciated the inevitability of radical change and became its midwife; the latter accepted that apartheid, whatever its injustices, could not forcibly be overthrown by the non-White population and that South Africa could not prosper at the price of White dispossession or annihilation. They struck that bargain and stuck to it and for this the country owes them much. This bargain was likewise accepted by the mass of the population irrespective of race and this was evinced by the queues which formed all over the country to vote on 27 April 1994, people of all races chatting with one another as if the previous 46 years had never been.[10] Irrespective of what happens in the years ahead, that event alone should offer hope.

The time has now come to consider the political situation that has evolved in the five states of Southern Africa which have achieved majority rule in the past three decades – Angola, Mozambique, Zimbabwe, Namibia and the Republic of South Africa – as well as the three former High Commission territories of Botswana, Lesotho and Swaziland which gained their independence rather earlier in the late 1960s. Though these countries are very different in terms of size, population and economic resources, an attempt will be made to find common political denominators between them and to predict possible political scenarios for them in the years immediately ahead.

## Angola

Angola became independent in 1975 and currently has a population of 12 million. It also has great wealth in terms of oil, coffee and diamonds and possesses some of the finest fishing grounds of any of the African littoral states. Sadly, war has since impeded the proper development of these resources – at any rate until recently.

Even before independence, Angola had been engaged in an attritional war of liberation against the Portuguese which was brought to an end by the Alvar Accords of 1975. Angola's problems, however, did not end with Portugal's departure: for the remainder of the 1970s, and well into the 1980s, the country's MPLA government had to counter rebellion from within by Jonas Savimbi's UNITA movement, a rebellion in turn assisted by South Africa from without. South Africa occupied much of the southern part of the country in alliance with Savimbi. Not until South Africa was militarily defeated at Cuito Cuanavale in June 1988 did this assistance come to an end. This defeat led to the subsequent Tripartite Conference of later that year, whereby the Soviet Union and Cuba agreed to disengage from Angola provided that South Africa agreed to implement UNSC 435 and permit free elections in Namibia. Gorbachev's attitude was, of course, crucial in this whole regard,[11] and South Africa was more than willing to withdraw from a position she could no longer readily hold.

Despite this withdrawal, the war continued between the MPLA and UNITA (still in control of most of southern Angola) until it was suspended, albeit temporarily, by the Bicesse Accords of 1991. These were brokered by Portugal, the Soviet Union and the United States and provided for a ceasefire, a 75 per cent reduction in the size of the UNITA army, the formation of united Angolan armed forces (the Forças

Armadas Angolanas or FAA), the restoration of central government authority in those areas controlled by UNITA and multi-party parliamentary and presidential elections for September 1992. This peace process was to be supervised by the parties themselves and monitored by a joint Politico-Military Commission established under UN auspices and actively assisted by the 'brokering' states. In the event, the Bicesse Accords were aborted because Savimbi refused to reduce his army in accordance with its provisions and progress with the establishment of the FAA was much too slow, only being completed a few days before the September 1992 elections. All this while, the two sides retained sizeable armies of their own.

The parliamentary elections, which were certified by the UN as 'free and fair', went decisively against Savimbi. Nevertheless, he refused to accept them, alleging malpractice by his MPLA opponents and, without even waiting for a run-off of the presidential elections in which the MPLA had failed to gain an overall majority, relaunched the war.[12] Though he was soon driven out of Lobito and Benguela on the coast, he seized much of the interior of the country, particularly in the south, where most of his traditional support lay. The subsequent civil war, which lasted over two years, involved enormous human suffering – the displacement of some three million people and sexual abuse of women on a grand scale.

Despite receiving considerable logistical support from President Mobutu of Zaire and despite his control of the main diamond-producing areas of Angola, Savimbi failed to maintain his initial geographic and strategic advantage over the MPLA. The latter succeeded in regalvanising itself on the back of greatly increased oil production in the period 1992–4, which meant greatly increased revues from oil tax. With them, the MPLA government was enabled to consolidate and fully equip the FAA. It was this national force which, by the end of 1994, had succeeded in blunting the military power of the UNITA army and thereby producing stalemate. Savimbi was thus persuaded, albeit reluctantly, to come to an accommodation with the MPLA. In November 1994, the Lusaka Protocol was signed[13] which again, for a time, brought hostilities to an end after a war in which some 300,000 people had been killed and much material damage done. But it also bought time for Savimbi. Tony Hodges' recent work *Angola: Anatomy of an Oil State* provides an invaluable guide to this whole situation.

The Lusaka Protocol included all the provisions of the previous Bicesse Accords but, unlike the latter, provided for power-sharing, the postponement of further elections until all its provisions had been fully implemented and the establishment of a UN peacekeeping force,

UNAVEM II, to oversee and enforce the peace process. As in 1991–2 after Bicesse, UNITA again dragged its feet and the timetable for the pacification and demobilisation of UNITA forces fell ever further behind. The elite units immediately around Savimbi were not reduced at all and most of the 70,000 UNITA 'troops' sent to the UNHQ to be 'demobilised' were soldiers in name only, being mainly reservists and sundry peasants. However, the UN chose to believe that this demobilisation was genuine and gave UNITA a clean bill of health for complying with the peace process, despite the fact that by mid-1997 it had still failed to cede authority to the MPLA in many areas under its control as stipulated by the Lusaka Protocol. At the same time, the UN substantially reduced its UNAVEM II force, originally 7,000 strong, to a mere 1,500 observer force.[14]

This prevarication by UNITA extended into 1998, during which time it continued to strengthen its control over much of southern Angola in open defiance of the Luanda government. The UN now realised the extent of UNITA's prevarication and, by Resolution 1173 of June 1998, banned the sale of Angolan diamonds which did not hold a government certificate of origin. However, this came too little and too late and finally, in December, the MPLA government lost patience and called on the UN to withdraw for failing to secure implementation of the Lusaka Protocol. Thereupon it marched against UNITA.

At first, the war went badly for the government, but gradually it succeeded in getting the better of UNITA. There were a number of reasons for this. Firstly, UNITA was handicapped by ongoing UN Security Council sanctions imposed over 1997–8 both over the sale of illicit diamonds and over flying rights for freight aircraft to UNITA-controlled areas (by Resolution 1127 of August 1997). Secondly, the recovery of oil prices during 1999, from their low point of 1998, meant that there was more money available for Luanda to spend on the FAA, which as a result succeeded in pushing the UNITA forces ever further east. Thirdly, there were many in UNITA who disagreed with Savimbi's eternally intransigent attitude to Luanda and the movement split two – and later three[15] – ways in the course of 1999. This led to the demoralisation of the whole movement and the desertion of many of its soldiers and indeed officers. Fourthly, the UNITA retreat eastwards meant that they increasingly lost control of the diamond-producing areas and, in consequence, of their principal capital base. Furthermore, UNITA was under international sanctions – which the MPLA was not. In sum, the movement came under the simultaneous pressures of political fragmentation, economic attrition and military harassment by the FAA, against which even the charismatic and mercurial Savimbi could not prevail.

With many of his troops starving, Savimbi was finally killed in an ambush in February 2002 and, shortly afterwards, his deputy Antonio Dembo succumbed to diabetes through getting cut off from his supplies of medication. The deaths of Savimbi and Dembo proved fatal to the already stricken UNITA and within weeks the leadership of its three factions requested peace terms from the MPLA government in Luanda. Early in April 2002, a 'memorandum of understanding' was agreed between the two sides: this provided for the implementation of the Lusaka Protocol, the disbandment and demobilisation of what remained of Savimbi's UNITA army and the incorporation of many of its former men and officers into the FAA. This laid the basis for the general reconciliation which has been taking place since 2002.

With the cessation of hostilities, what problems now remain? Clearly, an enormous amount of effort still needs to be devoted to repairing the ravages of a war which has afflicted the country for some 40 years both as colony and as independent state. Firstly, as a result of the 1992–4 and 1998–2002 hostilities, something in excess of three million people have been internally displaced; in other words, rather more than a quarter of the population. Many of them, the women especially, bear both the physical and the psychological scars of this process and have lost land which is traditionally and rightfully theirs. Secondly, some 10 million mines were laid by the rival armies during this period 1998–2002 and until and unless these are cleared agricultural production will be severely impeded and travel around this country will be unsafe.[16] Thirdly, the country's natural resources are going to have to be marshalled and accounted for in a much more systematic and disciplined fashion than they have been in recent years, and this is especially true of Angola's oil wealth, much of the taxation monies of which have never seen the light of day as far as the inland revenue authorities have been concerned. In 2002, Transparency International reported Angola to be the fourth most corrupt country in the world in its Corruption Perceptions Index for that year, despite the strictures delivered by President Dos Santos on the subject at the MPLA Party Congress in 1998:

> Citizens, workers and public officials resort to a series of illicit acts such as fraud, influence-peddling, bribery and the use of public monies to obtain advantages of a personal nature. Corruption is a worrying problem which must be stopped by measures of a legal and police character if we are not to lose complete control of it.

However well intentioned, these words seem to have had little effect in view of Transparency International's unfavourable report of 2002 cited above. Lack of transparency in public affairs is not something unique to Angola, but characteristic of the Third World generally, nor indeed are states of the developed world entirely without fault in this regard. In the case of Angola, however, the situation is particularly serious in view of the amount of oil money which has simply disappeared in dealings between Sonangol (Angola's National Fuels Company), the Central Bank of Angola and the Angolan treasury. It is difficult in the final analysis to avoid the conclusion that these monies have simply been siphoned off into the pockets of those in high political places, who have ready access to them. Though this allegation is strenuously denied by the present government, none of this money has since 'reappeared' and if the aspirations of President Dos Santos are to become a reality, vigorous and condign action at the highest levels of government is called for.

At this juncture, any observer of the Angolan political scene sees through a glass darkly. In a certain sense, Angola only became truly independent in 2002 with the ending of the war against UNITA and the death of Jonas Savimbi. Between 1975 and 2002, most of the earnings from oil and diamonds had been spent on armaments to sustain internecine warfare between the MPLA and UNITA. This war, in turn, involved the displacement of much of the population,[17] the arbitrary sowing of mines, the corruption of government at all levels and the spread of the HIV/AIDS virus amongst the population generally. Most public servants working in the provinces did not receive regular salaries, which resulted in a decline in morale and a severe deterioration in the standard of services. Sadly, this situation continues today.

What is now called for in Angola is a fresh start, a tabula rasa. The period 1975–2002, whilst it cannot be forgotten, must be put aside as any kind of political or economic model for the years ahead. Despite its abandonment of the one-party state in 1991, the Dos Santos government has retained at Luanda a highly centralised political system which does not sit easily with the multi-party democracy it is purporting to create. Nor does it sit easily with the many regions of the country or with the multiplicity of ethnicities within it. The various political parties which have emerged since 1991 do not yet adequately reflect the views of the groups making up the post-colonial state. To a great extent, civil conflict in the country has impeded this process but the parties which have emerged have few deep roots or consolidated institutional bases and often depend on alliances between political personalities. In constitutional terms, Angola is, by virtue of its size and diversity, much more suited to a federal than to a unitary system and this is arguably the direction in which the Dos Santos government ought now to endeavour to go.[18] It might also try to achieve a greater transparency and accountability in the management of its vast economic resources (notably oil) since the manifest shortcomings in this regard are not only derogating from the country's development but also lowering its reputation as a place in which honest business may be done. In the period 2002–4, both international aid donors and potential investors have been frightened away[19] by a fear that large sums of money will simply disappear without trace because of the absence of adequate accounting and audit systems in the public sector; the UN Consolidated Appeal Fund for Angola has had to be cut by almost a third following a lack of response from international donors and three-quarters of the 115 projects for which Luanda sought international funding have received none at all. The problem of HIV/AIDS has already been mentioned and will clearly need to be addressed, but perhaps even more important in the longer term is a general lack of education, which remains a legacy from Portuguese rule. Currently, only 25 per cent of Angola's female population are literate and this has implications both for resolving the AIDS problem and for the rearing of Angola's children, who can only benefit if their mothers manage to become educated. If the several problems mentioned in this paragraph can be addressed, the peace Angola has enjoyed since 2002 will perhaps be consolidated and the country's wealth, ably and honestly managed and fairly distributed, will enable it to move towards 'the broad, sunlit uplands'. In the meantime, however, there is much work to be done.

## Namibia

Namibia achieved its independence in April 1990. Once a colony of imperial Germany, it passed under the control of South Africa as a League of Nations mandate by the Treaty of Versailles in 1919 following Germany's defeat in the First World War. Thereafter it was administered to all intents and purposes as a province of South Africa. After the formal demise of the League in 1945, South Africa refused to recognise the United Nations as its legal successor and to make reports to it on Namibia's political or constitutional development. In 1966, the UN General Assembly passed a resolution condemning South Africa's 'illegal occupation' of the territory, but this South Africa ignored. Only with the collapse of Portuguese colonial power in Angola in 1974–5 did this situation begin to change.

Encouraged by this, the South West African People's Organisation (SWAPO) invigorated the guerilla campaign which it had begun in the early 1960s to compel South Africa to relinquish the territory. This campaign, whilst enjoying the political and logistic support of the Soviet

Union, was slow to bear fruit, but nevertheless constituted a thorn in the side of South Africa, of which its government over the years became increasingly aware and to which it had to devote significant military resources to counter. For about a decade, whilst accepting, in principle, UN Security Council Resolution 435, which called for the decolonisation of Namibia, it refused in practice to implement it – on the ground that its security would then be directly threatened by the Cubans and the Soviets from Angola. It was only after Mikhail Gorbachev came to power in the Soviet Union in 1985 and a few years later abnegated Soviet strategic interest in Africa generally that South Africa, under pressure from the US and the EU, felt able to accept Resolution 435 in its entirety and unblock the path to Namibia's political freedom. Over 1989–90 she vacated the territory and permitted the holding of free elections under international supervision, the country finally becoming independent on 21 March 1990.

Since then, SWAPO has maintained, indeed increased, its political dominance in government. In the elections of 1990, it won some 67 per cent of the total vote, its main rival, the Turnhalle Democratic Alliance (DTA) polling only 29 per cent. Four years later, in 1994, SWAPO polled 72.7 per cent of the vote whilst that of the DTA slipped to only 20.5 per cent. There is reason to believe that the DTA became demoralised by its impotence before the size of the government majority even before 1994 and that this demoralisation was mainly responsible for its poor showing in that year's poll. By comparison with SWAPO, the party was not well organised and its programme made little appeal even to its traditional supporters, most of whom were White and who had supported it as the governing party in the 1970s and 1980s when SWAPO was a proscribed organisation. By 1994, the wheel had come full circle: SWAPO were the masters and unambiguously so. This parliamentary primacy continued through the 1990s: in 1999, SWAPO retained the support of 72.5 per cent of the electorate, whilst that of the DTA shrivelled to a mere 11.7 per cent. The only cloud on the horizon for SWAPO was the Congress of Democrats (DC), formed in the previous year by younger and more radical elements of SWAPO who had become disaffected with the conservative nature of the party leadership. It was led by one Ben Ulenga, who had formerly been leader of the Mineworkers Union and Namibia's High Commissioner in London. After only one year of existence, it polled 12.1 per cent of the votes cast – indeed somewhat more than the DTA.

SWAPO's primacy was rather less evident at the regional and local levels. In the 1998 elections to local councils, 45 in all, SWAPO won 27 of them, whilst the several opposition parties won 16 between them and two were won by associations of local residents. This would indicate that genuine political debate is rather more in evidence in the regions than at the national capital, Windhoek, where SWAPO is the undisputed hegemon. A further factor contributing to the democratic spirit is Namibia's upper house of parliament, the National Council. Its strong SWAPO membership notwithstanding, it has not hesitated to criticise the government for lack of urgency in progressing land transfer policy and providing welfare support services in rural areas. A lively atmosphere also tends to prevail in the lower chamber, the National Assembly, where the opposition parties are granted the same amount of time and scope as SWAPO in determining the parliamentary agenda and there is no lack of opportunity to criticise.

All these features, of course, are most encouraging for the evolution of a genuinely democratic system of government in Namibia, but some words of reserve, caution even, are in order. After 1994, President Nujoma tended increasingly to centralise government and enlarge his own functions, as evidenced by his assumption of both the defence and the security ministries. His cabinet colleagues pursued this same tendency in the execution of their own portfolios and SWAPO retains in organisational terms the iron discipline which characterised it in its Marxist-Leninist days prior to independence. This discipline was resented by many of the younger elements in the party and feeling grew that the party leadership was failing to give fair consideration to alternative policy suggestions emanating from the lower echelons. This prompted the breakaway in 1998 and the emergence of the Congress of Democrats.

Rather more disconcerting – though perhaps not unconnected with the foregoing – was the tendency of the Nujoma administration to be hostile to criticism coming from the media. In 1996, the government sought to pass the Privileges and Immunities of Parliament Bill, which would have severely restricted reportage of all policy matters until they were officially announced. Had this gone through as originally proposed, it would have limited constructive discussion of important matters of public policy. After a storm in parliament, the most objectionable features of the bill were substantially modified, but the incident indicates the sensitivity of the government to non-parliamentary criticisms. In 1999, moreover, following criticism of the government, the Namibian Broadcasting Organisation was brought directly under the control of the president's office, Nujoma having accused the NBO of 'serving the enemy'. Similar charges were levied against other journalists who had penned articles critical of the government, and in 2002 Nujoma banned the NBO from broadcasting foreign programmes altogether, saying that they were 'corruptive of Namibian youth'. These various incidents inevitably cause one to question the extent of Nujoma's democratic bona fides. Similarly, he evinced his hostility towards the independent newspaper, *The Namibian*, in 2000 by withdrawing all government advertising from it and, the following year, banning all government departments from purchasing the paper at all, because he took exception to its tone and the manner in which it criticised government policy.

Another controversy concerned the amending of the constitution to enable the president to run for a third term in office. Under the constitution of 1990, the president was limited to two terms, which would have meant his standing down in 1999. However, in 1997, he decided, partly perhaps from personal choice, partly as a result of 'pressure' from political colleagues, to seek a third term and this was duly approved by SWAPO's annual conference that same year. In 1998, given the size of SWAPO's parliamentary majority, an amendment was readily passed in the National Assembly enabling this to happen, and in 1999 Nujoma duly embarked on his third term as president. The matter was (and perhaps remains) controversial because it involved a major amendment to the country's constitution very early in its history as an independent state and many argue that this should not have happened, as it set a most undesirable precedent and one which might be abused by a future incumbent less balanced than President Nujoma. Be that as it may, he came to the end of his third term and did not seek a fourth.

So, how can one sum up his 15 years as Namibia's first head of state? Firstly, he strictly observed the letter, if not perhaps always the spirit, of the independence constitution. He ensured fair treatment of the opposition parties in parliament as per the Westminster model, perhaps even more so. Debates in the National Assembly were lively and facilitated constructive discussion: the government accepted the need and desirability of criticism of its policies. However, this toleration of criticism did not extend to either the state or private media. The latter were expected to be very restrained in their criticism; if they were not, they felt the heavy hand of the state and were made to feel that they were 'the enemies within'. This derogated, naturally, from the democratic atmosphere to which the government had, since 1990, claimed to have been committed.

Secondly, Nujoma's government took pains to ensure that a fair balance of jobs and offices was struck between Namibia's various tribes. Of these, the Ovambo in the north were the largest and most sophisticated; it was also the tribe to which Sam Nujoma belonged. But Nujoma well perceived that stability could only come about if the largest tribe did not invariably get the lion's share: the balance he struck was largely accepted by the mass of Namibians even if occasional grumbles emerged from certain quarters. Indeed Nujoma was criticised for following this 'national reconciliation' policy too slavishly and in the process neglecting important areas of policy – such as land, unemployment and the AIDS pandemic – in other words putting a Herero into a ministerial post for the sake of political balance when an Ovambo might have been better qualified. The posts of prime minister, speaker of the National Assembly and secretary-general of SWAPO went to a Damara, a Herero and a Damara again respectively. That said, the presidency, the trade and industry ministry and the key army officer posts all remained the preserve of the Ovambos – and, to date, this has been accepted by the generality of Namibians including the smaller tribes.

Thirdly, the Namibian Defence Forces have kept themselves out of politics despite the fact that their variegated composition – former SWAPO freedom fighters and former members of the South West African Defence Forces when Namibia was under the control of Pretoria – might have rendered this a problem. However, irrespective of their differing antecedents, the military has remained loyal to the Namibian state and it is vital that this should continue.

As Namibia has recently embarked on its second phase as an independent state under the leadership of Hifikepunye Pohamba, it is important that the latter should ensure that the same kind of tolerance which Sam Nujoma has inculcated into the parliamentary system should equally be found in the civil society and that the harassment of the media, which sadly characterised the last years of Nujoma's rule, should become a thing of the past. No state which purports to be a democracy can deny the legitimacy of a free press and remain credible. It would indeed be sad if the high standard of political tolerance in Namibia to which the Helen Suzman Foundation paid tribute in 1997 was, over time, to be found wanting.[20]

## Mozambique

When the Armed Forces Movement (the MFA) revolted against Lisbon in April 1974, there was one dominant nationalist movement in Mozambique – the Front for the Liberation of Occupied Mozambique (FRELIMO) – and it was to FRELIMO that power was transferred by the departing Portuguese in the course of 1974. This did not occur smoothly, an attempt being made by conservative Portuguese settlers to abort the process, and the period September–October of that year saw turbulence and much loss of life both Black and White. This prompted a mass efflux of Portuguese settlers, who sabotaged residences and industrial installations as they left, and within two years only 10 per cent of the original Portuguese population remained. At the same time, the primacy of FRELIMO in government came to be established at the capital, Maputo. This, it should be noted, was in stark contrast to the situation in Angola, where power was being contested by a nationalist movement split three ways.

The first few years of FRELIMO rule saw considerable socio-economic and political progress. Secondary-school enrolments rose from 20,000 in 1974 to 94,000 by 1982. A vaccination programme launched in 1975 had, by 1980, successfully immunised some 96 per cent of the population against tetanus, smallpox and TB. Between 1975 and 1985 the number of primary health care centres available to the population doubled, as did primary-school enrolments. A national literacy campaign was launched in 1975 which succeeded in increasing the general level of literacy by 20 per cent in five years – from, admittedly, abysmally low levels under the Portuguese. Sadly, for Mozambique, these early years proved to be the false dawn of a better day.

There are a number of reasons why this progress was not maintained. Firstly, the country could not, in the long term, sustain the loss of skilled and qualified personnel occasioned by the Portuguese efflux of 1974–6. As the 1980s went on, fewer and fewer primary schools, especially in the north of the country, functioned properly, due to a shortage of sufficiently qualified teachers, with the result that 95 per cent of children were failing to pass the first four grades of primary school on time. Secondly, much of the land vacated by the Portuguese had been taken into public ownership and state farms established on them in accordance with the terms of FRELIMO's Marxist-Leninist doctrine. These farms too lacked properly qualified managers and the cost of running them had been underestimated. Insufficient tools were available and many peasant farmers originally happy to work on them became disillusioned and drifted back to their own small farms; sometimes they got away with this, at others the FRELIMO authorities took severe reprisals. Thirdly, this unsatisfactory and unproductive situation was exacerbated by adverse weather conditions during the period 1977–82, initially floods in many parts of the country followed in the early 1980s by severe droughts. These caused a precipitate fall in both agricultural exports and cereal production and the government had to import food to avert massive starvation.[21] This caused many from the countryside to come into the towns of the south in search of work which was not to be had. Following presidential strictures about 'idle people cluttering up the towns', FRELIMO simply deported those who were unemployed or could not prove their permanent residency to the remote provinces of the north in the expectation that they would work in agricultural concerns there. This press-ganging of large numbers of people to parts of the country they did not know (very reminiscent of Portuguese practice in colonial times) and for agricultural work of a kind they were not necessarily used to (known as 'Operation Production') did not succeed in its objective and simply made the FRELIMO government very unpopular. All this rendered Mozambique's internal economic situation extremely parlous. However, on the political and diplomatic front, worse was to come in the form of South Africa's destabilisation policy which began in 1980 and was directed at SADCC's five 'front-line' states, of which Mozambique was one, and spearheaded by RENAMO as South Africa's proxy.

RENAMO, the National Resistance Movement for Mozambique, was founded in 1976–7. It consisted of a variety of alienated people – residual Portuguese settlers, Africans who had profited under Portuguese colonial rule, disaffected adherents of FRELIMO and those affected by FRELIMO's 'push-and-shove' policies just described. Ideologically, at least at first, they had little in common apart from an intense dislike of FRELIMO: by 1979, Afonso Dhlakama had emerged as the de facto leader of this motley but ruthless band.

It was supported at the outset by the Smith regime in Rhodesia, which clearly had every interest in undermining the FRELIMO government in Maputo because of its support for Robert Mugabe's guerilla army. But this support, active until 1979, ceased after the Lancaster House Agreement of December of that year and the subsequent independence of Rhodesia as Zimbabwe. From 1980 onwards, however, South Africa under the leadership of President P.W. Botha sustained RENAMO with munitions and logistical support. Botha's object was to weaken the FRELIMO government and thereby to discourage it from giving assistance to the guerrilla forces of the ANC which it had been doing since its accession to power in 1975. Apart from helping RENAMO with munitions, South African security forces would operate incognito through surprise attacks on houses suspected of harbouring ANC activists, causing as much aggravation as possible to Mozambique in the process. Paul Nugent, in his recent book *Africa since Independence*, has provided a valuable insight into this conflict.

RENAMO constituted a thorn in FRELIMO's flesh from 1976 onwards, and increasingly after 1980 when it had South Africa's support. Initially, it operated against FRELIMO by a guerrilla campaign of unalloyed brutality against the civilian population, including maimings and rape. In regard to strategic targets, it moved against the Nacala–Maputo railroad and the Umtali–Beira oil pipeline, causing the maximum possible disruption.[22] Its activity against people was most brutal in the south, where FRELIMO's hold was strongest. In the centre and north, where it was less dominant, the RENAMO bands temporised much more and even endeavoured to win the hearts and minds of the people in these regions. Whenever possible, they tried to make political capital out of FRELIMO's 'villageisation' and 'Operation Production' policies which had proved so unpopular amongst those who had been sent up from the south. But, overall, RENAMO's policy, particularly before the Nkomati Accords of 1984, was one of brutalisation of the civilian population and terrorisation of those who had escaped the worst atrocities. The appearance of the former in villages minus ears, lips or breasts made a certain impression on the minds of the latter. Cooperation with RENAMO might just possibly make discretion the better part of valour.

This appalling situation was gradually transformed after the 1984 Nkomati Accords. By these, the South African government reached a deal with FRELIMO, whereby it would cease its support to RENAMO on the understanding that Maputo would in turn cease hers for the ANC by sheltering its members on her territory. This deal profited both sides: President Samora Machel could not otherwise control RENAMO and for President Pieter Botha the failure of the Tricameral Constitution and the subsequent unrest in South Africa's townships meant that the power and political appeal of the ANC had to be diminished as much as possible. Though breaches of the Nkomati Agreement occurred on both sides, its general effect was to bring about a cooling of the situation, as RENAMO could no longer rely on the unqualified support from South Africa which it had enjoyed in the first half of the decade. Though it continued with its campaign of violence in the south, this was at a diminished level, and in the centre and north it did conduct a quasi-democratic campaign, however crude, for the hearts and minds of citizens. It capitalised on the harshness of FRELIMO's domestic administration, its villageisation policies and its incessant criticisms of Mozambique's tribal chiefs, who were generally far more popular than the FRELIMO government chose to suppose. All this had the effect of wearing FRELIMO down and the death of its leader, the highly charismatic Samora Machel, in an air crash in 1986 served only to accelerate this process. By the end of 1986 RENAMO was making political gains in many parts of the country.

However, it was not only in Mozambique that the political situation was changing. At the higher strategic level, events were on the march. From Moscow in 1987–8, Gorbachev let it be known to all his African protégés that the Soviet Union was 'calling in its loans' and that military assistance to the MPLA in Angola, SWAPO in Namibia and FRELIMO in Mozambique and concomitant diplomatic support would no longer be forthcoming. This removed the impasse in Southern Africa which had pertained since the collapse of the Portuguese empire in 1974. It also caused South Africa both to soften its political stance towards FRELIMO and to further diminish its links with RENAMO, a process already begun under the 1984 Nkomati Accords. Yet even more significant were the political changes in South Africa itself at the end of the 1980s.[23] P.W. Botha's replacement as president by F.W. de Klerk in 1989 marked a sea change in South Africa's policy towards its neighbours to the north. Pretoria now felt that it had bigger fish to fry: Botha's 'destabilisation' policy gave way to one under de Klerk of moving towards a political accommodation with the African National Congress via negotiations with the still incarcerated Nelson Mandela. Whilst all this was in progress, the Berlin Wall came down in Germany in November 1989, setting in train a series of events which, by the end of that year, had brought about the demise of all the Communist regimes in Eastern Europe and called distinctly into question the general credibility of one-party states.

For FRELIMO, these developments were highly significant. Though no longer under direct pressure from South Africa, she had lost her principal ally in the USSR, and RENAMO, though no longer supported by South Africa, had achieved a life of its own in both political and military terms and was challenging for primacy in the centre and north of the country. After considerable diplomatic manoeuvring and not a little 'persuasion' by external powers, notably South Africa, the UK and the Soviet Union,[24] FRELIMO renounced Mozambique's position as a one-party state and adopted a multi-party system in November 1990. Despite this, there were no negotiations with RENAMO and the war continued, albeit in a condition of stalemate for both protagonists.

This situation continued for almost two years and might have lasted even longer but for the drought of 1992, which gravely affected both sides. RENAMO's grain and water supplies in the areas under its control ran down, causing widespread hunger and dislocation; in the south, a similar situation prompted widespread desertion by common soldiers from the FRELIMO army. Both sides had no longer the will or the means to continue the war, and this was recognised by their respective leaderships by the middle of 1992. Under the auspices of the United Nations and the European Union, they came to an accommodation and a formal peace accord was signed at Rome in October 1992. By this, the FRELIMO and RENAMO forces were to be disbanded and reintegrated into a national army of 30,000 men,

RENAMO was to be recognised as a legitimate political party and free elections were to be held in October 1993 (in the event delayed until October 1994). The accord of 1992 held good, because of the interest taken in it by leading members of the international community and the UN. The Security Council agreed to supply a 7,000-strong peace-keeping force (UNOMOZ) to supervise both the demobilisation of the combatants and the 1994 elections. The USA agreed to finance and retrain RENAMO as a constitutional political party and RENAMO renounced its terrorist past, enabling it thereby to participate in the 1994 elections. Other UN agencies and international religious groups agreed to educate the Mozambican public in the importance of elections, democratic practices and the rule of law generally. Subsequent to the accords, an investment programme was established, to which Portugal, South Africa and the UK have been the main contributors: such a programme was vital in view of the economic destruction and dislocation that the war had occasioned.[25]

In the election of October 1994, there was a turnout of just over 87 per cent, which was greatly encouraging in a nascent democratic system, FRELIMO gaining 129 seats to RENAMO's 112: in the accompanying presidential race between President Joachin Chissano (FRELIMO) and Afonso Dhlakama (RENAMO) the share of the vote was 53.3 per cent and 33.7 per cent respectively. In the next elections in 1999 the gap separating the two parties in terms of parliamentary seats was broadly the same, whilst the presidential elections showed a much narrower gap of barely 5 per cent between Chissano and Dhlakama.[26] This serves to illustrate the importance of personalities in African politics, in that voters tend to identify themselves more strongly with charismatic leaders than with party programmes. Otherwise, proportional to the parliamentary results, the gap would have been some 19 per cent rather than a mere 5 per cent. These figures reflect a total turnout in 1999 of only 69.5 per cent.

Several conclusions in Mozambique's politics can be drawn from this. Firstly, there has been a decline in electoral turnout between 1994 and 1999, but the figure of 69.5 per cent remains a good one by Western standards. Secondly, the narrowness of the presidential lead in the 1999 elections was challenged by RENAMO, who demanded a recount under the Constitution, but this was refused by the Supreme Court of Mozambique. Although this gravely displeased RENAMO, they did not defy this decision – which bodes well, as do the continuing high turnout figures at elections, for the future of Mozambican democracy. Thirdly, Mozambican local government procedures, when set against those of central government, appear rather parlous. Although local government institutions and the power of chiefs are guaranteed under the 1990 Constitution, there is, at present, a good deal of variance between the regions as to how local government and the power of chiefs work in practice, and this is something which in the longer term could be exploited by RENAMO to FRELIMO's detriment. It therefore behoves the latter to work to ensure that any glaring anomalies or ambiguities are removed. Fourthly, due very largely to American assistance, RENAMO would seem to have made the transition from guerrilla movement to political party successfully; this is not merely good in itself but constitutes a precedent which might be emulated in the future.

At present, therefore, the future for democracy in Mozambique seems set reasonably fair. In 2001, President Chissano announced that he would be stepping down from office in 2004 and Armando Guebeza, who had been elected to the post of secretary-general two years previously, duly succeeded him in December 2004, following elections which gave FRELIMO a substantial parliamentary majority over RENAMO.[27] However, the question must inevitably be raised as to whether RENAMO will be prepared to accept its role as opposition party – perhaps for a considerable time – or whether its early history will at some stage prompt it to return to war. This latter outcome will, hopefully, not pertain; since 1992, there has been a substantial increase in civic development, with the creation of women's groups, human rights groups and land tenure groups, which are all in a position to lobby the government with their opinions either directly or by way of a press which is largely free of government constraint. Apart from RENAMO's future political stance, the only issue giving cause for concern is whether 12 years is sufficient time for a democratic system to take root and be properly appreciated by the citizen body. There is a tendency at present for democracy to be equated in the public mind with socio-economic factors – that is, better public services, growth in prosperity and the absence of unemployment. Things like minority rights, the rights of opposition parties and the rule of law remain a closed book to most. Such an appreciation may take not merely years but decades fully to develop.

## Zimbabwe

On 18 April 1980, just 90 years after the Union Jack had first been raised in Salisbury, Zimbabwe became an independent state under the leadership of Robert Mugabe. This had been heralded by the Lancaster House conference in London during the autumn of 1979, at which Britain's foreign secretary, Lord Carrington, chaired discussions on Zimbabwe-Rhodesia's political future with the country's principal political actors:

Ian Smith of the Rhodesian Front, Bishop Abel Muzorewa of the United Africa National Congress (UANC), Robert Mugabe of the Zimbabwe African National Union (ZANU) and Joshua Nkomo of the Zimbabwe African People's Union (ZAPU). After some 13 weeks of discussion, terminating in December, the coalition government of Zimbabwe-Rhodesia (of which Smith and Muzorewa were the leading members) announced its repudiation of Rhodesia's UDI of November 1965 and its acceptance of elections based on universal adult franchise. Before the month was out, Prime Minister Margaret Thatcher appointed Lord Soames as governor of Britain's last African colony and tasked him with overseeing its transition to independent statehood.

This task was undertaken by Lord Soames with both skill and vigour. To the ordinary people of Zimbabwe-Rhodesia, he stressed that their vote would be both free and secret; for those who had fought against the former White regime, he organised, with the cooperation of the Black political leadership, the time, terms and conditions under which they should hand in their arms. Happily his bone fides were accepted and the elections of February 1980, held under international Commonwealth supervision, passed off as well as could be expected, despite allegations that ZANU had resorted to intimidation, which should arguably have been further investigated by the Commonwealth observers. In the event, victory went to Robert Mugabe's ZANU, which polled 57 seats to the 20 polled by Joshua Nkomo's ZAPU, the Rhodesian Front polling 20 and the UANC of Bishop Muzorewa three. Thereupon, Lord Soames called upon Mugabe to form a government: this the latter proceeded to do, his large majority notwithstanding, in coalition with Nkomo's ZAPU, believing that this would minimise friction between Zimbabwe's two principal tribes and contribute to the country's unity and stability. Mugabe believed, in this initial period, in the importance of achieving political consensus by way of discussion, debate and compromise.

This approach might just conceivably have worked, but for the mutual antagonism of these two men's personalities and their historic rivalry for the political soul of Zimbabwe. Though both had been imprisoned under the Smith regime between 1963 and 1974, they were then released and, thereafter, led the nationalist struggle against the regime, Nkomo from Zambia and Mugabe from Mozambique. Mugabe's campaign was much more effective than Nkomo's, with the result that he captured the hearts and minds of the people in a way which Nkomo did not. This was demonstrated in the election result of February 1980 and there is little doubt that this rankled considerably with Joshua Nkomo.

In terms of temperament also, the two men were very different. Nkomo was a 'larger-than-life' character, flamboyant, expansive, open and alto-gether more charismatic than the cool, calculating and more introverted Mugabe. Irrespective of their tribal allegiances (Mugabe's Shona people of the north and east jostled uneasily with Nkomo's Matabele in the south and west), the two men tended to clash in cabinet discussions on political issues generally. These clashes were compounded by the histor-ical differences between their two tribes and the budgetary allocation of resources between Matabeleland and Mashonaland. However, Mugabe coexisted with Nkomo as his deputy for nearly a year, demoting him from the vice-presidency in 1981 to the post of minister without port-folio and finally expelling him from the cabinet altogether in 1982. This set the scene for the turbulence which was to characterise the next five years of that decade, for the Matabele did not take kindly to Nkomo's ejection from the government. Mugabe, however, felt strong enough to do this, in view of the size of his ZANU majority; he also felt, as prime minister and perhaps not entirely unreasonably, that it should be he and not Nkomo who was calling the shots.

To a people already smarting from their leader's departure from gov-ernment, Mugabe then delivered a further body blow through an edict calling for the Shona language to be used as the principal teaching medium in primary schools after the age of seven. This infuriated the Matabele, who rose in revolt against the Shona-dominated government in 1983, and Mugabe dispatched thither his army's Fifth Brigade, trained in North Korea in counter-insurgency tactics. The revolt was put down over the next 12 months with singular ruthlessness and brutality, and it is esti-mated that some 20,000 Matabele perished as a result of the activities of the Fifth Brigade. Mugabe vilified the Matabele for 'fomenting violence' and implicated Nkomo in this. So threatening did the political situation become for Nkomo that he was eventually forced to flee abroad and, from the relative safety of Europe, castigated Mugabe for the way in which he was running the country. Throughout the mid- to late 1980s, the country remained in turmoil until finally, in 1987, Nkomo and Mugabe agreed to bury the hatchet and to unite their two parties into ZANU-PF. Nkomo realised that he did not have the political strength to prevail against Mugabe, but equally Mugabe came to the conclusion that he could not tolerate Matabele irredentism as a festering sore within the body politic. Be that as it may, the unification of the two parties was an agreement very much in Mugabe's favour: Nkomo's political career as leader of ZAPU came effectively to an end, but he did nevertheless receive half a loaf as vice-president of Zimbabwe, shorn though this post was of significant political power. The 1988 rapprochement largely restored the political situation which had pertained at independence seven years earlier.

The period 1980–7 is instructive in regard to the controversy surrounding President Mugabe's more recent career. At the outset, he appeared to be genuinely inclusive by including Joshua Nkomo in his government: within two years, however, he had demoted and later dismissed him out of personal dislike rather than for the reasons stated. His subsequent handling of the disturbances in Matabeleland is further evidence of this: he would not brook political opposition and brutally repressed it when it came. The rapprochement of 1987–8 indicated a return to a more consensual approach.

The merging of ZAPU and ZANU-PF into one mass party introduced into Zimbabwe politics a degree of apparent quietism but, beneath the surface, all was far from well. This merger had the effect of diminishing the size, strength and variety of opposition groups. In the parliamentary elections of March 1990, ZANU-PF won 116 of the 120 seats in the House of Assembly, one went to Abel Muzorewa's UANC (a survivor from the last days of the illegal regime) and two went to Edgar Tekere's ZUM (Zimbabwe Unity Movement). Tekere had only formed this party the previous year, after being expelled from ZANU-PF for constantly criticising government policy, and so had little time to establish ZUM as a credible entity. He was also politically tarred by his previous association with ZANU-PF and the voters thus felt that they had little by way of genuine political choice and showed their disenchantment by staying away from the polls in large numbers. ZANU-PF's victory in the 1990 elections was secured on a poll of only 54 per cent of those eligible to vote and a similar result emerged at the 1995 elections. These latter were also boycotted by a further eight opposition parties, which had emerged during the period 1990–5, on the ground that their supporters had encountered intimidation in the run-up to the elections from 'elements of ZANU-PF'. This was the first time, though sadly not the last, that such allegations were to be made against the governing party. Irrespective of the truth of these, the generality of the Zimbabwean electorate felt alienated from the whole political process for three reasons: firstly, the overweening power of ZANU-PF; secondly, the paucity of genuine choice between the opposition parties; and, thirdly, a universal sense that MPs, feeling that they had their jobs for life, cared little for the grievances of their constituents and only showed their faces in their constituencies on the approach of elections.

This disillusion with the political process on the part of ordinary Zimbabweans went hand in hand with their growing discontent at their socio-economic situation. In 1995, the country had been independent for 15 years: during that time, however, little had happened to secure a significant transfer of resources from White to Black. The situation regarding ownership of land remained very much as it had been in the days of the UDI and before. Though the Mugabe government had done much to improve Black access to education generally and secondary education particularly, the number of jobs available to secondary-school leavers was sadly deficient. In 1995, there were only 30,000 jobs available for the 200,000 qualified secondary-school leavers seeking them. The unlucky 170,000 simply added to the statistics of the unemployed, became to a greater or lesser extent a burden on their families or, in the unhappiest cases, were encouraged to resort to crime. This all served to make discontent with the government of Robert Mugabe pervasive. In the presidential election of 1996, the latter polled 92 per cent of the vote, but only 31 per cent of the electorate actually voted. This was hardly a situation from which he could draw satisfaction, so he began to search for ways by which he might become more popular, whilst maintaining the virtual monopoly of power which he had built up over the years through the vehicle of ZANU-PF. One of the ways chosen was the indigenisation of the economy, notably the land-ownership issue, the other was the question of a new constitution.

Over land, the government's original intention had been to resettle 200,000 African families on 'reclaimed' land: that is, land that had been vacated by Whites on a 'willing seller, willing buyer' basis. About a third of the country, on independence, was in the hands of 4,800 commercial farmers (mainly White) and contained the best-irrigated land in the country. But progress in reaching the 200,000 target remained slow: by 1995, some only 50–70,000 families had been resettled on former European land, principally those who had rendered 'guerrilla services' to ZANU during the bush war against the Smith regime and others who had ingratiated themselves with ZANU-PF by dint of political loyalty. This had served to whet the appetite of the majority not fortunate enough to have been resettled, who much resented their continuing dispossession. In August 1997, the government took steps to address this situation, allowing war veterans substantial 'unbudgeted benefits' in the form of further grants of land as more Europeans vacated their land – it must be emphasised that at this stage there were no compulsory sales or expulsions. Whilst a minority benefited from these land grants, the majority remained unassuaged, but a start, however slight, had been made in redressing the economy in favour of the Blacks.

The other matter related to the Constitution. This had essentially been determined in 1979 at Lancaster House as a result of negotiations between the British, the (then still illegal) government of Zimbabwe-Rhodesia, ZANU and ZAPU. It was never approved by the people of Zimbabwe as a whole after independence. During the 1980s and 1990s, pressure gradually built up for changes in the constitution, which for some time the government ignored, even though many in the middle and lower echelons of ZANU-PF wanted them. By 1998, pressure over the constitutional issue had built up sufficiently for the leading elements of civil society to come together in a new body, the National Constitutional Assembly (NCA), to challenge peacefully and constitutionally the structure of state power which had been allowed to develop since 1980. The NCA was organised by the Zimbabwean Council of Churches (the ZCC) but also comprised the Zimbabwean Congress of Trade Unions (ZCTU), the Zimbabwean Union of Journalists (ZUJ), the Zimbabwean Human Rights Association (Zimrights), the Zimbabwe Catholic Commission for Justice and Peace and a number of other groups, all concerned about the manner in which political power was being exercised by ZANU-PF. These groups debated with one another about how to make the Zimbabwean constitution more democratic and more transparent: significantly, the NCA secretariat was chaired by one Morgan Tsvangirai, the secretary-general of ZCTU.

The ZANU-PF government, having rejected suggestions for change in the Constitution over many years, was alarmed by this development. In October 1998, it launched its own constitutional initiative, broaching changes which would have consolidated its position still further. Mugabe offered dialogue with all interested parties at this time including the NCA, but, although some brief contact between them took place, it soon became clear that there was no meeting of minds. Soon afterwards even these discussions ceased, following the suppression by the riot police of pro-reform demonstrations by elements sympathetic to the NCA. Mugabe then appointed an election commission with orders to draft a new constitution, but many of the 395 original appointees subsequently withdrew when they perceived the legalistic constraints under which President Mugabe was placing them and the extent to which their own judgement was being circumscribed. Even the commission's report, when it finally emerged in the latter part of 1999, reflective though it was of the government's position in most respects, was subsequently scrutinised by a ZANU-PF cabinet committee to close any loopholes whereby the government might yet be challenged: indeed the president was to be empowered under its terms to amend the constitution unilaterally if he saw fit. So, over the period 1998–9, there were two sets of mutually antagonistic constitutional discussions in train – those of ZANU-PF and those of the NCA under the aegis of these various civic organisations, of which Morgan Tsvangirai's ZCTU was one of the most prominent. Throughout 1999, the atmosphere became ever more fraught, Tsvangirai formally entering the political arena in October of that year by setting up a new opposition party, the Movement for Democratic Change (MDC). The stage was now set for ZANU-PF to be challenged in a way it had not previously experienced.

In November 1999, the government published its proposed constitution, which had been drawn up in an atmosphere of singular isolation, and shortly afterwards announced that it would be submitted to a referendum in February 2000. When this was held, only 26 per cent of the electorate actually turned out, 54 per cent of them voting to reject it. This was a severe setback for the ZANU-PF government and a distinct snub to President Mugabe personally. ZANU-PF's confidence in him as leader faltered and questions started to be raised about whether he was not becoming an electoral liability. Mugabe was well aware of these rumblings and exceedingly concerned as to how to re-establish his popularity. His defeat in the constitutional referendum of February 2000 marks the point at which he resorted to the arbitrary and extra-constitutional tactics for which he has since been so much criticised. As such, it is a key date in Zimbabwe's recent political history.

Following Mugabe's defeat, a number of things happened in quick succession. First, the president let it be known to his 'war veterans' that if they occupied White farmland forcibly, the authorities would not intervene. This the war veterans proceeded to do and the unfortunate White farmers appealed, to no avail, to the police authorities, who had been ordered 'to stand idly by'. During the month of March alone, 800 European farms were taken over: there was no case of financial compensation being paid to those dispossessed and insult was added to injury by a constitutional amendment[28] of April 2000 that those dispossessed should apply to the former colonial power for compensation. Second, Morgan Tsvangirai's MDC came in for active harassment by ZANU-PF and there was a sustained campaign for disruption of their activities whenever possible, a campaign which has continued ever since. Third, this same period saw the continuation of the government's campaign against *The Standard* newspaper for defamation: its proprietor, editor and one of its leading journalists were arrested and tortured on a number of trumped-up charges.[29] These arrests had originally been made in 1999 and only in May 2000 were the accused absolved of any wrong-doing by the Supreme Court of Zimbabwe and released.

In June 2000, elections were held nationwide for the House of Assembly. On this occasion, they were more universally supported – probably by virtue of there being more meaningful opposition presence in the shape of the Movement for Democratic Change. Despite the incidence of considerable intimidation of voters by the government the MDC polled 47 per cent of the electoral vote and gained 57 seats; ZANU-PF polled

48.6 per cent and achieved 62 seats and ZANU (Ndongo), a breakaway splinter party from ZANU, achieved just one seat. A team of UN election monitors who had been sent to observe polling withdrew following obstruction by government officials and the government refused to grant entry visas to 200 foreign election monitors. By comparison with the parliamentary elections of 1995, the political scene in Zimbabwe had been transformed. Government and opposition were now running neck and neck. This was, of course, gall and wormwood to President Mugabe. His response was to increase government pressure on both the White farmers and the MDC, who were in his eyes becoming increasingly synonymous. In July, he announced that a further 500 White farms would be taken over – without compensation – and soon afterwards, in September, the MDC offices in Harare came under hand-grenade attack. Slight though the damage was, the perpetrators have never been discovered and just how vigorously the police authorities have since pursued them remains a matter of conjecture. In December, President Mugabe made a further speech about the country's White population, castigating them as 'the enemies of Zimbabwe.' These various incidents all serve to indicate that 2000 was the year, following his defeat in the constitutional referendum, when Mugabe decided to go it alone in political terms, regardless of either domestic or international opinion. This trend continued during 2001: at the Commonwealth Conference at Abuja in Nigeria in September 2001, Mugabe's land seizures attracted much unfavourable comment and he gave an undertaking that these would cease, but this promise was never subsequently kept and the invasions continued into 2002. Indeed between March and September 2002, 3,300 'commercial' farms were taken over, which brought 85 per cent of former European farmland into that available for redistribution to the Black population.

Apart from these seizures of commercial farmland, 2002 also witnessed the passage of domestic security legislation reminiscent of South Africa's apartheid period. In January, the Public Order and Security Act banned the publication of documents designed to provoke disorder or undermine the security services as well as prohibiting the holding of public gatherings which might result in rioting. This act gave wide discretion to the authorities to be judge of the circumstances, as had pertained in much of the security legislation of South Africa in the 1960s and 1970s. The other measure, passed at this same time though subsequently ruled unconstitutional by the Supreme Court, was the General Law Amendment Act, which prohibited foreign monitoring of Zimbabwean elections. The government had been particularly keen to do this in view of its intimidation of the MDC ever since its establishment in 1999. Indeed in February the leader of the EU's electoral mission team was expelled from the country as a result of it, an expulsion which caused the EU to take sanctions against the Zimbabwean government in the form of an arms embargo, the suspension of £125 million worth of aid and the banning of all visits by government ministers to any EU member state. At the same time, Morgan Tsvangirai was formally arraigned on a charge of treason (for allegedly plotting to assassinate the president) though released on bail pending trial and permitted, albeit reluctantly, to continue with his political activity.

In the presidential elections of March 2002, Mugabe, Tsvangirai and three others competed for the presidency: Tsvangirai gained 42 per cent of the vote and Mugabe 56.2 per cent. The MDC alleged governmental harassment of its supporters and this allegation was confirmed by the Commonwealth Election Monitoring Force[30] which even Mugabe had hesitated to ban. Subsequent to the elections, Zimbabwe's membership was suspended mainly on account of these irregularities, though partly following its refusal of a Commonwealth suggestion that a government of national unity be appointed. Mugabe baulked at the idea of sharing power in any way with Tsvangirai, who was now facing a charge of treason.

Encouraged no doubt by his success in the presidential elections, Mugabe continued his campaign of repression. Not only did the farm seizures continue, but on 15 March 2002 a further measure was passed by the House of Assembly, the Freedom of Information and Right of Privacy Bill. This decreed that all journalists would require accreditation by a specialist government panel before being allowed to publish anything, thereby enabling the government to silence any reporter of whose opinions it disapproved.

In February 2003, just a year after being initially charged with treason, Morgan Tsvangirai again found himself before the High Court in Harare, though the trial was adjourned in May and resumed later in the year during which time he remained on bail. Throughout he contested the charges, giving evidence in his own defence in January 2004. Eventually, in October, Judge Paddington Garwe acquitted him on the ground that the prosecution had quite failed to substantiate its charges and also commented unfavourably on the flimsy and unsatisfactory evidence of much of the prosecution's case.[31] The government snarled but had no other choice than to accept the verdict of the court, muttering threateningly that it did not regard this matter as finally closed and that further evidence would be sought. Its attempt to 'nail' Tsvangirai by way of the judicial process had completely failed.

All this time, the economic situation had rapidly deteriorated – largely due to the seizures of the commercial farms by veterans and the inability of those thereafter in possession to farm them properly or indeed at all. The government had a policy for transferring the ownership of land, but no policy on how it should remain productive, no thought given to the training of the new owners in agricultural techniques and no resources to help them purchase the right capital equipment. The result was widespread famine and some of the worst sufferers were those who had previously been employed as labourers on European farms, some 1.5 million in all. During 2003, the government was compelled to accept food aid to alleviate this problem but even then insisted that the final responsibility for distributing this aid to affected areas should rest with ZANU-PF. In August of that year, International Human Rights Watch accused the government of channelling this to those areas (mainly the rural ones) supportive of ZANU-PF and by the same token depriving the urban areas (where support for the MDC was strong). Thus even food aid became a political weapon in the whole Zimbabwean imbroglio. The government treated the former employees of the European farmers particularly harshly, doing their utmost to ensure that they received little or no food aid. This and similarly oppressive behaviour decided the next Commonwealth Heads of Government Meeting (CHOGM) at Abuja in Nigeria in December 2003 to suspend Zimbabwe's Commonwealth membership indefinitely.[32] President Mugabe withdrew his country from Commonwealth membership before the suspension could come into effect.

How does Zimbabwe's political balance sheet now stand? It is hard to be other than lugubrious about its present situation or its immediate future. Only a decade ago, in 1995, Zimbabwe was one of Southern Africa's greatest success stories. Its agriculture was sufficiently advanced and efficient to enable it to feed not only itself but much of the rest of the region as well. This was due to its commercial sector, which was basically in the hands of White farmers, who understood the business of farming and whose presence had been welcomed by President Mugabe himself upon his accession to power in 1980. The latter appreciated very well the importance of a continuing European contribution to Zimbabwean agriculture, realised indeed that his country could not do without it: the bargain struck was that the Whites could remain, farm and prosper provided that they kept out of politics. This bargain held for two decades, not seriously breaking down until the constitutional referendum of early 2000. During those same two decades, with the notable exception of the ZANU–ZAPU friction of the 1982–3 period and the subsequent upheavals in Matabeleland over the next three to four years, the political situation in Zimbabwe remained reasonably quiescent, certainly sufficiently so as not to attract unfavourable comment from the outside world. Throughout this time, ZANU-PF remained dominant and this dominance remained unchallenged until the very end of the 1990s, a situation which perhaps largely accounts for this high degree of quietude.

The position is now very different. President Mugabe's takeover of the White commercial farming sector from 2000 onwards has caused a massive decline in such commodities as maize and tobacco, on which the country had previously relied for both domestic consumption and export earnings. This policy has in turn led to the neglect and spoliation of the land, for those Africans who subsequently acquired it have neither the skill nor the capital resources to farm it productively and the government has no policy for remedying matters. Land has become a political totem, White possession of it being regarded as 'wrong' and Black possession of it as 'right'. Bad though this situation is for the White farmers (only 600 of whom now remain of the original 4,800), it is even more devastating for the 1.5 million of their Black employees who, at a stroke, have lost both their jobs and their homes on what had hitherto been European land. The fact that they have been, often for years, in European service has done nothing to endear them to the ZANU-PF government.

On the political front, the dominance of the latter has been severely eroded. In 1998, this government encountered its first challenge from Zimbabwe's civil society in the emergence of the National Constitutional Assembly, which had as its prime objective the modification of governmental power. It needs to be remembered not only that ZANU-PF had an extremely large majority in the House of Assembly but also that it had inherited at independence a highly centralised machinery of government dating from UDI and before.[33] This gave it formidable powers which many felt should be diluted in constitutional terms: the NCA's proposals over this did certainly not come as music to the government's ears. Even more serious for the Mugabe administration was the formation of the Movement for Democratic Change in 1999 by Morgan Tsvangirai. This had the support of urban-dwellers, industrial workers, the intelligentsia and, to the extent that they were politically active, the Whites. Mugabe's reaction to the emergence of the MDC was not unlike his response to the Matabeleland disturbances of 1983. Rather than parley or negotiate with it in a proper democratic spirit, he sought to harass it at every opportunity and smash it if he could. There is every evidence that the various démarches made in the period after February 2000 had government approval, if not indeed active government instigation. Tsvangirai's success at the subsequent parliamentary elections in June only added to President Mugabe's ire and hostility. It is highly arguable that, but for the electoral malpractices that took place during both this 2000 election and the presidential election in 2002, the MDC would now be in power and Tsvangirai would be president. On the diplomatic and international front, these same malpractices and the endeavours of the Commonwealth and the EU to see that they were properly addressed resulted in sanctions being taken against Zimbabwe by the EU, and then the US, and the suspension of her Commonwealth membership until she mended her ways. It is something of a Faustian path that Zimbabwe has trodden, and not one that in earlier years could reasonably have been foreseen.

Finally to President Robert Mugabe himself. Exactly what kind of man is he? His record and his reputation are often in conflict. He has been reported as a man constantly in search of consensus,[34] yet his recent acts would rather suggest the opposite. Whilst imprisoned in Rhodesia between 1963 and 1974, he rose to become de facto leader of his fellow prisoners and, as a former schoolmaster, gave them tuition on literacy and political organisation. He taught them that, in resolving problems, it was important to seek consensus. Following his election victory of February 1980, he asked Nkomo and ZAPU, his sizeable parliamentary majority notwithstanding, to join him and ZANU in coalition in the belief that this would smooth the political passage of Zimbabwe's early years. The fact that this coalition broke down was largely due to personality differences between the two men, but Mugabe deserves credit for the attempt and again, in 1987, he mended fences with Nkomo and made him one of his vice-presidents. All these actions are those of a reasonable and democratically inclined man prepared to bargain and compromise. There is, however, a darker side: he could not tolerate opposition as evidenced by his policy of repression in Matabeleland in 1983, when literally thousands of people, many of them women and children, perished at the hands of the Fifth Brigade. During the years 1987–98, when he faced little political challenge, all was quiet, but the moment the MDC was formed in 1999, it came in for persistent and vicious harassment by the authorities which would never have occurred in a truly democratic country. This included the intimidation of voters in both the 2000 parliamentary and the 2002 presidential elections and Mugabe's cavalier attitude towards the EU election monitors only serves to indicate his contempt for the whole electoral process. Not only did ballot boxes disappear prematurely from the urban areas (where the MDC was strong) but they also remained on well after official closing time in rural areas (where ZANU-PF was dominant). Worse even than this rigging was the physical intimidation of MDC voters throughout the country, by war veterans and members of the Zimbabwe Youth

League, both solid adherents of ZANU-PF and acting with the full connivance, if not on the orders, of the leadership. Morgan Tsvangirai was arraigned in 2002 on two charges of high treason; one of these finally failed in 2004 but the other remains outstanding and will put him in danger of his life if it succeeds. Journalists critical of the regime and judges of the higher judiciary who have overruled the government in the courts have both been the subject of substantial official pressure, with threats of imprisonment (sometimes carried out) for the former and of forced or early retirement for the latter. These are not the acts of a benign regime.

In a valuable recent article,[35] Professor T.E. Ranger describes President Mugabe as a 'driven' man. Ranger argues that Mugabe views Zimbabwean history though a prism of three *chimurengas*; that is three revolutionary upheavals. The first was over a century ago when the Matabele king, Lobengula, was cheated of his land by the Whites under Cecil Rhodes and then defeated when he tried to resist; the second was the war of liberation against the Smith regime in the 1970s in which he played so signal a role and ultimately prevailed. But that did not suffice for Mugabe, who is intensely ideological and messianic and sees it as his duty, in a third *chimurenga*, to extirpate what remains of White influence and economic power in the country. Thus will Lobengula be finally avenged and Zimbabwe, under his leadership, will move rapidly towards 'the broad, sunlit uplands'. Africans will regain the lands lost so tragically by Lobengula all those years ago and, for this, the Whites will pay the price today. Mugabe prays that God may yet spare him a few more years to ensure the success of this third *chimurenga*. The tragedy of this is that it is a fantasy in the mind of the president. Far from advancing, his country is in outright retreat, its economy in disarray, many of its people unemployed and starving and its diplomatic reputation in tatters, and all the while political terror stalks the land. All this could have been avoided had President Robert Mugabe been less concerned with his place in Africa's history and more concerned with making Zimbabwe 'a lead player' in the current development of Southern Africa.

## South Africa

The year 1994 witnessed the final demise of apartheid and the advent of majority rule based on universal adult suffrage. This represented a sea change in South African politics, given the White hegemony which had prevailed since independence in 1910 and which had in turn been buttressed by the multi-faceted policy of separate development after 1948. Even the White population was for the most part prepared to trust the political transformation so skilfully engineered by F.W. de Klerk of the National Party and Nelson Mandela of the ANC. The election of April 1994 saw the ANC emerge as by far the largest party, with 62.7 per cent of the national vote. The National Party (NP), the founder of apartheid and still strongly supported by most of the White population, polled 20.4 per cent and the Inkatha Freedom Party (IFP), strong in KwaZulu Natal and led by Chief Gatsha Buthelezi, 10.5 per cent. Nelson Mandela, leader of the ANC, had already seen the wisdom of trying to forge a government with as broad a consensus as possible and so April 1994 ushered in 'a government of national unity' in which all these parties were represented and in which all their leaders held important portfolios, F.W. de Klerk and Thabo Mbeki each holding the two posts of deputy president and Gatsha Buthelezi that of home affairs minister. On that apparently hopeful basis, the new South African ship of state was launched.

There were, however, both storms and rocks ahead, even if they commanded little attention in these early heady days: 'Bliss was it in that dawn to be alive, / But to be young was very heaven!' [36] The government of national unity was not in fact particularly united and indeed there were strains within the ANC itself – primarily on the question of how the economy should be managed. There was tension too between Nelson Mandela and F.W. de Klerk: the latter felt that his National Party was not being given enough influence relative to its size and withdrew it from the 'grand coalition' in May 1996 after just two years of collaboration, refusing to countenance further the principle of 'power-sharing' under the new permanent constitution which was at that time under discussion. He argued, perhaps understandably, that power-sharing militated directly against the creation of a viable parliamentary opposition. There had, too, been growing friction between the ANC and the IFP over the administration of KwaZulu Natal, notably the extent to which political power should be devolved from Pretoria to Durban. It is hardly an exaggeration to say that Chief Buthelezi did not rule out the secession of KwaZulu Natal from South Africa in the event of failure to agree on the general principle of devolution. Whilst in the event it did not come to this, it added to the tensions within the government.

Turning to the tensions within the ANC, these related to the overall management of the economy, particularly whether the emphasis should be on redistributing national resources in a more equitable way or expending those same resources without undue concern for equality. The first trend was represented by the Renewal and Development Plan (RDP), which had its philosophical antecedents in the 1955 Freedom

Charter, which was socialistically inspired and to which the young Nelson Mandela had then given his voice. He saw Black–White economic inequality as something which would be diminished and formally excised by centralised planning in which government would have a key role. The principal objective would be job creation in all areas of the economy, so that Blacks would come to escape the poverty and uncertainty of perpetual un- or underemployment and slowly but surely see the economic tarpaulin being ratcheted upwards in their favour. Orthodox economic disciplines, such as control of the money supply, would not hold pride of place. This policy, which was broadly one of 'tax and spend', dominated ANC thinking during the run-up to April 1994 and for nearly two years after independence. It was eventually abandoned in March of 1996.

The second trend of thought was quite different and involved adherence to strict financial practices more redolent of the developed world. Orthodox financial management was 'in', 'tax and spend' according to the whim of government was 'out'. The argument was that if South Africa was to build its economy upon a rock rather than upon sand, control of the money supply was crucial. This meant such things as balanced budgets, wage-control policies, privatisation and judicious use of interest rates. Sadly, too, it meant in the short term fewer rather than more jobs, but, more optimistically, it meant the attraction of more investment monies from abroad which would lead to the broad expansion of the South African economy and, in the longer term, to generally enhanced prosperity. It would, however, be 'jam tomorrow' and be unlikely to happen very quickly.

Nelson Mandela, whatever his earlier predilections for the RDP, became converted during the first two years of his presidency to this second trend of thinking. His conversations with the governments of the OECD countries led him to realise that South Africa could not 'walk tall' in a rapidly globalising world – nor perhaps even in Africa – if it did not play to a considerable extent by the book and embrace fiscal and monetary procedures which had stood the test of time. It was borne in upon him that, failing this, foreign direct investment would be unlikely to be forthcoming in significant quantities and, in consequence, that South Africa would not soon escape this disturbed economic legacy she had inherited from the apartheid period. Moreover, many of his colleagues within the ANC had spent years in exile in such countries at Zambia and Tanzania and witnessed the unreliability of their centrally planned economics. They did not want a similar pattern to develop in South Africa. So Mandela, strongly supported by his vice-president Mbeki, came down on the side of economic orthodoxy.

The Renewal and Development Plan was formally abandoned in March 1996 – to be succeeded in June by the Growth, Economic and Redistribution Plan (GEAR).

This volte-face was by no means generally welcome to members of the ANC. Many argued that they had joined the party in the first place because of its adherence to socialist economic principles and that these were now being jettisoned as a result of pressure from the developed, capitalist world. They opined that they had not fought against the capitalism of apartheid only to see it replaced by another, even one marginally less obnoxious. They wanted national resources redistributed, they wanted inequality diminished, they wanted an economic as well as a political revolution. Winnie Mandela, once Nelson's wife, and Peter Mokaba, the ANC Youth League leader, were in this camp, as was the South African Communist Party (SACP) and the Confederation of South African Trade Unions (COSATU). Both these organisations had traditionally been supportive of the African National Congress when it was a 'liberation party' and indeed this support continued after 1994 when the ANC became dominant in government. It did, however, become increasingly qualified, because neither of them saw the problem of economic inequality being adequately addressed and this was especially true of COSATU, which represented the Black working class much more directly than did the SACP, which was supported primarily by the radical intelligentsia, both Black and White. In COSATU's counsels the question was increasingly raised as to whether it could continue to support the ANC politically when its 'orthodox' economic policies seemed to be damaging its members' vital interests. This is evinced by the fact that at the end of 1998 over 30 per cent of the South African workforce remained unemployed (or uncertainly employed in the informal sector) and that the 560,000 jobs which needed to be created annually to combat this were not forthcoming. Though a political revolution might have taken place in 1994, the economic revolution had yet to come. This was, however, a minority feeling within the ANC, troublesome though it was to the leadership. The prestige of Nelson Mandela was not to be withstood and the election of 1999 was fought (and won) on the primacy of GEAR. However much some regretted it, there was to be no return to the RDP. Indeed, at that election, the ANC increased its share of the vote from 62 per cent to 66 per cent and Thabo Mbeki, always a staunch supporter of economic orthodoxy, became president. He has since continued to plough the furrow initiated by Mandela.

A few words must now be said about both the Truth and Reconciliation Commission (TRC) and the Constitutional Court (CC). The TRC was established by an Enabling Act in June 1995. As its name implied, its purpose was to expose the fullest possible truth about apartheid, basically murders and crimes of violence committed in the context of that, and thereby to achieve a measure of reconciliation between perpetrators and victims. The victims could tell their stories and, at the commission's discretion, be awarded compensation; perpetrators could confess their deeds and apply for amnesty with the promise that, if this were granted, no further action would be taken against them.

Overall, the whole process could not be said to have been entirely successful. The adjudications were not always seen as fair, the NP, the IFP and the PAC coming off generally less well than the ANC, and all the political parties boycotted the final publication of the commission's report on the ground of unjustified criticism. On the positive side, much truth about the apartheid system came to light and the White population was generally aghast about much of what had been done in its name.

There is perhaps a certain analogy here between the Truth and Reconciliation Commission of 1996–8 and the Nuremberg War Crimes Tribunals of 1945–6 in that in each case much of the evil of apartheid and Nazism respectively was exposed to public view. But just how much reconciliation between the races occurred, in the light of the relatively small number of prosecutions of those who had not been granted amnesty, remains a matter of conjecture.[37] But it is perhaps important that a certain 'beating of breasts' should have taken place in the interests of proving beyond reasonable doubt the evil of a system known by some and suspected by many. Alex Boraine, the deputy chairman of the TRC, in a remarkable book,[38] has written of it establishing 'a process' rather than aiming at a formal, finite goal; he stresses that reconciliation can only truly come about if the socio-economic gulf between White and non-White be manifestly diminished.[39] 'Reconciliation' needs a sheet anchor in 'restitution' if it is not to drift away on the ebb and flow of the political seas.[40] It needs both this and a calm recognition of the evil which has gone before – and a willingness, in the words of Nelson Mandela, to 'let bygones be bygones'. Those who remain reluctant to forgive should remember how much and how long their first president suffered. Perhaps the last word should remain with the London *Times*, which stated in an editorial of 31 October 1998,

> The critics [of the TRC] – Black and White – have claimed that truth has been emphasised at the expense of reconciliation. This argument cannot be sustained. It would have been inexcusable to censor incriminating material simply to avoid embarrassing South Africa's past and present leaders. Any attempt at such an exercise would have rightly led to a charge of political bias. It is hard to see

how a litany of lies could serve as the foundation of meaningful reconciliation. No committee can ever resolve the horrors of past atrocities. They can point towards a more civilised future – and in this case they have done so.

The Constitutional Court came into being in February–March 1995. Its role in South Africa's political evolution is not dissimilar to that of the Supreme Court of the United States in determining that country's destiny. Its duty is to ensure that parliament passes no law which is in conflict with either the Constitution or the Bill of Rights. In practice, it will secure the state against the dangers of majoritarianism, a consideration especially relevant at the present time given the size of the government majority. Soon after its inception, the court was asked by parliament to give an advisory opinion on the 'constitutionality' of capital punishment and whether this conflicted with the 'right to life' guaranteed under Section 3 of the Bill of Rights.[41] Another issue so referred was that of police access to privileged documents which are *sub judice*: easy police access might jeopardise the legitimate rights of accused people; difficulty of access might contribute to malefactors escaping justice altogether. Clashes between customary tribal law and the Bill of Rights is a further problem the court may increasingly have to consider, in that women's rights in South Africa, especially in the rural areas, are largely regulated according to customary law. The seven 'lay' judges which the president is empowered to appoint will therefore need to have a sociological and political awareness rather than a purely legal competence.[42]

Finally, in considering the ebb and flow of South African politics since 1994, several points seem to emerge clearly. The first is the continuing hegemony and parliamentary dominance of the ANC. No other party has remotely emerged to challenge it and, following the general election of April 2004, it currently commands 69.7 per cent of the popular vote from an initial base of 62.7 per cent ten years previously. Despite the problems of economic management already mentioned, the ANC has not fragmented as many predicted in the mid-1990s. It has remained a united party, though one representing a very broad church. Its dissentients have for the time being muffled their voices because they know they have nowhere else to go, though this situation could change if the economic and employment position fails to improve. The Pan-African Congress is too small, with only three seats in parliament, and too fraught with personality conflicts to command much support, and the Inkatha Freedom Party is more of a regional than a national party, commanding little support outside KwaZulu Natal.

The second is the fact that, despite the hopes of many on the advent of majority rule in 1994, South Africa's politics remain – and for the foreseeable future are likely to remain – very race-based. Dennis Worrall,[43] in the early 1990s, spoke of a time when South Africans would be able to debate and adjudicate political issues irrespective of race, but this has proved overoptimistic, if not indeed utopian. Basically, Blacks vote for the African National Congress and Whites for the Democratic Alliance, at any rate since the demise of the National Party in 1997. It is perhaps unrealistic to expect otherwise, given the extent to which race has always been the dominating factor in South African politics and the extent to which the wealth of the country has been concentrated in the hands of one rather than several races. The ANC, whilst always a non-racial party, has relatively few active White members and the Democratic Alliance relatively few African, Coloured or Asian, and these latter tend to be regarded as 'Uncle Toms' by their own people. This situation has to change if South Africa is to develop as a rounded and mature democracy.

The third feature, and one directly connected with the race-based nature of South African politics, is the weakness of the parliamentary opposition. The ANC is dominant with 279 seats in the South African parliament: it faces in the Democratic Alliance an official opposition party of 50 seats which is in itself in broad political alliance with the IFP with its 28 seats following an electoral pact made between the two parties in 2003. Whether the DA and the IFP have enough in common to be able to pose a credible and durable alternative to the ANC in terms of a policy programme seems extremely dubious, given the regional nature of the IFP and the national appeal which the DA purports to make. Helen Zille, leader of the DA since May 2007, will almost certainly have a different political agenda to Chief Buthelezi, leader of the IFP and until 2004 a member of Thabo Mbeki's cabinet, though the fact that he was not reappointed after the 2004 election may render an viable parliamentary alliance between the two parties more rather than less likely. The other political parties – the United Democratic Movement (UDM), the New National Party, the Pan-African Congress and the Freedom Front number only 23 seats between them and cannot even be considered a makeweight to the DA and IFP in oppositional terms. Such opposition as does exist in parliament must therefore come as much from dissentient voices in the ANC as from the DA or the IFP; however, as already stated, these voices are not strong and Mbeki's dominance as ANC leader is unlikely soon to be challenged, short of a major political upheaval at present unforeseen.

That upheaval might, however, come about as a result of the interplay of the following factors – the failure of the Black unemployment situation to improve significantly, the failure of land transfers from White to Black to materialise as promised in 1994[44] and the failure to instil a greater observance of law and order. There are currently some 3.76 million licensed cab-drivers in South Africa and over four million unlicensed ones: these latter form part of the 'informal sector' but are nonetheless breaking the law: this is just one of the problems which the government needs to address. Much more serious has been the great increase in criminal violence on the streets of South African cities and, perhaps most notably, in South Africa's Black townships. Rape of women and sexual abuse of children have already been mentioned, and the ready availability of firearms from the earlier conflicts in Angola and Mozambique has served the cause of criminals frighteningly well. These three problems are going to have to be addressed as a matter of urgency by the Mbeki administration during the years immediately ahead. To its credit, it has set its face against illegal land seizures, Zimbabwe-style, orchestrated by the PAC in 2001, though it has been far less successful in containing criminal violence generally. If both the unemployment and land situations were to ease, this could have only a favourable impact on the problem of criminal violence. If the present widespread criminal violence were to diminish, this would improve the chances of South Africa attracting foreign direct investment – which would in turn assist the refurbishment of its economic infrastructure and serve to diminish its level of unemployment. It is upon the ability of the Mbeki administration to gauge the interconnectedness of these three problems and to apply policies accordingly that its ultimate success will depend.

## Botswana, Swaziland and Lesotho

These three countries, known during colonial times as the High Commission territories, were British protectorates, achieving that status by formal petition to London late in the nineteenth century and early in the twentieth. Bechuanaland (now Botswana) and Basutoland (now Lesotho) came under British protection in 1885 and 1868 respectively and Swaziland somewhat later, in 1903. The native chiefs of the first two were anxious to avert the risk of being dominated by the Boers in the republics of Transvaal and Orange Free State and, likewise, the Swazi king, not wanting to see his country incorporated into an enlarged, White-dominated South Africa, was glad to accept British protection shortly afterwards. However, the British South Africa Act of 1909 did raise the possibility of these countries eventually becoming part of South Africa provided their inhabitants so consented. Though requests for the transfer of these territories to South Africa were made by Pretoria from time to time, that consent was never forthcoming due to the existence of apartheid and the three finally became independent in the 1960s, the final tranche of British African territories to do so.

Of these, Botswana has been by far the most successful. Though much of the country is desert, it is also endowed with much mineral wealth, mainly diamonds, and also considerable numbers of cattle which serve for the export of beef. It is, however, diamonds which provide its greatest resource and this has been exploited to considerable advantage in the years since independence in 1966, currently accounting for one-third of Botswana's GDP and for 70–80 per cent of its export earnings.[45] Indeed, it can be argued that the diamond industry has been overexploited and the agricultural sector correspondingly neglected, leaving the economy as a whole less rounded than it should be. That situation was exacerbated by a severe outbreak of foot-and-mouth disease in 2003 which reduced the number of cattle very considerably. Notwithstanding the success of the diamond industry, the country as a whole suffers from chronic unemployment, which has had political repercussions,[46] and also from AIDS, which has severely depressed the levels of agricultural production.

On the political front, the country has been governed sagely by all its presidents – Seretse Khama, Quett Masire and Festus Mogae – since its accession to independence. In 2003, its good governance and the calibre of its public bodies were praised by Transparency International and a tribute paid to its adherence to contracts and the rule of law. Political parties have consistently been allowed to flourish, although the dominance of the Botswana Democratic Party (the BDP) has never been seriously challenged. Nevertheless the politicisation of the country has been much assisted by the chiefly *kgotla* and freedom square meetings which occur at regular intervals throughout the country. The parliamentary opposition has always been numerically small and, since 1998, has fragmented into two parties, the Botswana National Front (BNF) and the Botswana Congress Party (BCP), which in the 1999 election gained seven seats to the BDP's 33. Since 2003, an attempt has been made by one Kenneth Koma to reorganise the opposition by way of a new party, the New Democratic Front, but how far this will be successful in challenging the BDP remains uncertain, especially as in the last elections of 2004 it only succeeded in polling 13 seats to the BDP's 44. In the longer term, the opposition will need to grow in both numbers and political stature if Botswana is to develop into a mature democracy.

Despite this overall good record, there are one or two wrinkles on Botswana's political canvas. Firstly, the San and the Bushmen have come under pressure from Gaberone to quit their ancestral lands in the Kalahari and discontinue their nomadic existence. This is partly because the government believes they should modernise and partly because it wishes to turn much of the Kalahari into a game park for tourists, which is crucial for foreign exchange earnings. The San and Bushmen have fought the constitutionality of these demands in the courts and a final outcome is still awaited. Secondly, there is an element of doubt about the manner in which President Mogae appointed Lt Gen. Ian Khama to the vice-presidency: this was done without any election either by the BDP or the electorate. This is a particularly sensitive issue as Khama, being a military man, has never experienced the cut and thrust of democratic politics, yet Mogae clearly intends to groom him for the presidency when he leaves office in 2008. Thirdly, when criticised by one Professor Kenneth Good, an Australian political science lecturer in the University of Botswana long resident in the country, over both the Khama appointment and the issue of the San/Bushmen land in the Kalahari, Mogae endeavoured to have him expelled at 48 hours' notice as a 'prohibited immigrant', but was temporarily thwarted in the courts; somewhat later, however, he was expelled. Such supersensitivity at presidential level does not bode well for political tolerance in Botswana and many fear that Khama, if elected president, would adopt the same line. A strong and united parliamentary opposition would be in some position to apply pressure on the government over matters of this kind, but this is something which Botswana does not yet have.

Unlike Botswana, Swaziland has a long tradition of political autocracy. Its first constitution, introduced by the British in 1964, granted the paramount chief, King Sobhuza II, full executive power; the second, bequeathed again by the British in the 1967–8 period during the run-up to independence, provided for a parliament and a 'first-past-the-post' electoral system. In the first elections, the king's party, the Imbokodvo National Movement (INM) gained all 24 seats in the House of Assembly, whilst the opposition, the Ngwane National Liberation Congress (NNLC) failed to win any, despite receiving 20 per cent of the popular vote. This result, brought about by the electoral system, caused a governmental domination of the House of Assembly which could hardly be described as reflecting the popular will. At the next elections, in 1972, the situation was hardly changed, though on this occasion the NNLC did gain three seats to the INM's 21.

Even this degree of opposition was anathema to King Sobhuza. The following year, 1973, he declared a state of emergency, ordered his party in parliament to repeal the Constitution and introduced legislation which provided for detention for a period of 60 days without charge or trial. All political parties were abolished, including his own INM, and parliament's role was reduced to debating government proposals and 'advising the king'. Members of Parliament ceased to be directly elected but were instead indirectly elected by the 40 traditional councils (the *tinkhundla*) by way of an intermediate electoral college. This, of course, served to distance parliament from the people and buttressed to an enormous extent the power of the king. Democracy in Swaziland was effectively 'snuffed out' by this emergency legislation of 1973.

King Sobhuza's death in 1982 did little to alter this situation. After a brief period of political confusion between 1982 and 1986, during which two queen regents ruled the country in the minority of Sobhuza's son,[47] Prince Makohosetive, the latter succeeded to the throne in 1986 at the age of 18. Once he had acceded, the new king, now Mswati III, showed his determination to continue in the autocratic tradition of his father. In 1986, he established a special tribunal to hear all cases of sedition against the throne or against the queen regents (which had taken place on frequent occasions between 1982 and 1986). No lawyers were to be permitted to appear on behalf of the accused parties and the only appeal from a decision of the tribunal lay to the king himself. It was hardly a system in which justice could be seen to be done.

All this while, royal hostility to the concept of political parties continued. The main opposition party, the People's United Democratic Movement (PUDEMO) was established illegally in 1983 during the period of political confusion between 1982 and 1986, though its existence was tolerated thereafter. In October 1990, however, it distributed pamphlets all over the country calling for constitutional reform and major changes to the monarchy. As a result, in November its leaders were jailed for some months without trial or charge: only international pressure secured their release in March 1991. Notwithstanding this, PUDEMO continued its campaign for a more open system of government, including the legalisation of political parties, which was anathema to the king: as a result, he announced his intention in 1992 of ruling by decree and was backed by the House of Assembly in this. PUDEMO was joined in its campaign by the Swazi Federation of Trade Unions (SFTU) and the Swazi Youth League (SWAYCO), both of which felt that the time for political reform had come, though the SFTU was more concerned to achieve a new framework for industrial bargaining than to secure the legalisation of political parties. In 1995, a list of 27 demands was drawn up jointly by the SFTU and SWAYCO and presented to the king, but to no great effect, the latter continuing to assert his own wisdom and presumption of 'divine right'. In June 2001, he issued a decree awarding himself wide and largely unsupervised powers and was only persuaded to rescind this the following month by the threat of trade sanctions from the USA.

To sum up, the political situation in Swaziland remains fragile and politics of the kind familiar in the US and Western Europe still seems a long way off. Though illegal, political parties are tolerated until they make a distinct nuisance of themselves; thereafter, their leaders face either the threat or the reality of imprisonment. In their favour, it must be said that they have never tried to achieve their objectives by violent or unconstitutional means, but it is clear that King Mswati III resents criticism of any kind. His regime is bizarre on points of detail: in 2001, attempts were made to compel all women under 18 to remain celibate and to avoid even shaking hands with men – this in an endeavour to combat AIDS which had been ravaging the country since the mid-1990s.[48]

His extravagance, too, for the ruler of a small, poor country is proverbial. The House of Assembly, normally fairly indulgent of royal requests, resisted his wish to purchase an aircraft for his personal use from the USA for US$45 million and also one to build individual palaces for each of his ten wives. This combination of political autocracy and personal extravagance rather reminds one of the late Sese Joseph Mobutu of Zaire and the fate he eventually came to. The most recent constitutional proposals (of 2003) remove the king's power to rule by decree; provided these are ratified and there is progress towards genuine democracy thereafter, Mswati may escape the fate of Mobutu.

Lesotho, formerly the British protectorate of Basutoland, achieved internal self-government in 1965 and subsequently elections were held which brought the Basutoland National Party (BNP) to power under the leadership of Chief Leabua Jonathan. It was this party which took Lesotho into independence in October 1966 with Chief Jonathan as prime minister and Moshoeshoe II as king.

Since independence, Lesotho's politics have lacked the openness and integrity of Botswana's but nonetheless succeeded in escaping the autocratic sclerosis of Swaziland's. The democratic structure bequeathed by the British has been preserved but not without difficulty nor without the active assistance of SADC in 1998. During this period, Lesotho has experienced civilian rule, military intervention, military counter-coup and allegations of election-rigging following the restoration of civilian rule in 1991.

The political ebb and flow within Lesotho has been determined largely by personality clashes between its various leaders rather than disagreements about policy. In the June 1970 elections, Chief Jonathan, when successfully challenged by Ntsu Mokehehle's rival Basuto Congress Party (BCP), declared the election invalid, temporarily imprisoned King Moshoeshoe and detained a number of the BCP leadership. This very much set the tone of the politics which was to follow: in 1974, Mokehehle was exiled and Jonathan embarked on a period of increasingly personal rule. This lasted until 1985, when he was removed by the army for provoking South African military intervention through his support for the ANC within Lesotho. His successor, Colonel Justin Lekhanya, suspended the democratic process, adopted a more conciliatory policy towards South Africa and successfully negotiated with Pretoria the Lesotho Highlands Water Development Project which, by providing South Africa with fresh water, earned his country much-needed foreign exchange. However, his dictatorial and abrasive style (he exiled King Moshoeshoe in 1991 following a disagreement over Military Council appointments) alienated even many of his own military colleagues and he was ousted from power in 1991 and succeeded by one Colonel Elias Ramamca.

Ramamca organised a return to civilian rule and elections were duly held in March 1993. However, the results of these were disputed due to the BCP winning all the seats in the House of Assembly, though gaining only 54 per cent of the vote: the BNP gained 16 per cent but won no seats. This produced tensions in the body politic which festered for several years, eventually leading to the demise of the BCP and Moke-hehle's resignation as prime minister (the latter had been able to return home to Lesotho after the eclipse of Chief Jonathan in 1985). Though he had succeeded in founding a new party, the Lesotho Congress for Democracy (LCD), he had lost too much prestige during the 1993–7 period to continue in leadership, which was then assumed by one of his old BCP colleagues, Pakalithi Mosisili. In May 1998, this party won the election with a substantial majority but the opposition parties alleged electoral fraud and nearly brought the government down and law and order with it. Mosisili appealed to SADC for military assistance. This was granted and a force of 800 men from South Africa and Botswana was sent to restore the situation.[49] This it did but not without bloodshed and Lesotho's opposition parties spoke of their country 'being invaded by SADC and South Africa'. In October 1998, the SADC establish-ment, consisting of a troika of South Africa, Zimbabwe and Botswana, decided that the May elections should be annulled and fresh elections held within 18 months; however, these could not take place within this timescale due to the tensions extant in the country. When they were finally held in May 2002, they gave Mosisili's LCD a renewed and substantial majority which rather implied that the 1998 elections had been fair after all. Since then, although he has presided over a country much affected by industrial unrest, famine and AIDS, democracy has at least been maintained and his government has enhanced its reputa-tion by standing firm against the corruption which has occurred over the Lesotho Highlands Water Project and bringing those responsible to book.[50] The current outlook is brighter than it has been since political activity was restored by Colonel Ramamca in 1991. The future rather depends on whether policies are allowed to compete openly with one another on their merits or whether the often dysfunctional personages who walk Lesotho's political stage will gain the upper hand.

In conclusion, these three former High Commission territories provide an interesting and varied patchquilt in political terms. In Swaziland, there is unabashed monarchical absolutism which seems likely to endure unless King Mswati III changes his attitude to the legitimacy of political parties or is removed by force majeure. His remoteness from his people, his personal extravagance and his resentment of criticism all contribute to this latter outcome. Lesotho's politics since independence have been a case of thrust and counter-thrust between the dominant personalities, both civil and military, not always with great regard for constitutional niceties and 'due process'. Nevertheless, with the help of its neighbours in SADC, parliamentary government has been preserved, despite the hiccups of 1993 and 1998, and the present government holds power on the basis of free elections last held in 2004. If (and it is a big 'if') matters improve on the socio-economic front, especially in regard to AIDS and chronic unemployment, the medium-term future looks not unpromising. Only in Botswana has the Westminster model been followed both in letter and spirit with both political parties and media being allowed to operate in a virtually untrammelled way and the country presided over by a highly competent civil service recruited on merit rather than patronage. The existence of regular political meetings throughout the country, based on the chiefly *kgotlas* and 'freedom squares',[51] does much to ensure that ordinary people participate and hence feel they have a stake in their country's political system.

## General conclusions

What conclusions, then, can be drawn about the political nature of Southern Africa based on this consideration of South Africa, Zimbabwe, Angola, Mozambique, Namibia and the three former High Commission territories? These must inevitably be provisional and tentative given the youthfulness of both the Namibian and South African polities and the fact that both Mozambique and Angola have but recently emerged from civil war; a number of common features do nevertheless emerge.

Firstly, the dominance of the political leader is crucial to an appreciation of how government in Southern Africa works. He is very much more than *primus inter pares*, dwarfing to a greater or lesser extent his various cabinet colleagues. This is particularly the case in those countries where the anti-colonial struggle has been long and bitter; rather less so where it has not. Thus, in South Africa, Nelson Mandela was an icon for disenfranchised Blacks well before his release from prison in 1990; thereafter, his position was reinforced by the readiness of the White government to negotiate with him the transfer of power. Likewise, in Zimbabwe, Robert Mugabe's leadership and eventual success in fighting a war of liberation against the Smith regime during the late 1970s ensured his triumph in the country's first free election in 1980 and his advent to power as president. The subsequent political eclipse of his main rival, Joshua Nkomo, and the merging of Nkomo's ZAPU with his own ZANU in 1988 ensured that he remained unchallenged for almost a decade thereafter and it was only the excesses of his rule which brought about political challenge by Morgan Tsvangirai's Movement for Democratic Change, a challenge nevertheless unsuccessful at the time of writing. In Angola, the MPLA did not finally succeed in asserting its authority over the whole country until the death of Jonas Savimbi, the UNITA leader, in 2002, which brought that organisation's resistance to Luanda finally to an end. Savimbi had successfully resisted the MPLA's authority since the Portuguese withdrawal in 1975 and dominated both UNITA and Southern Angola generally with singular ruthlessness and singular charisma. But for his death, it is probable that the MPLA–UNITA war would have continued. In Namibia, Sam Nujoma's leadership of SWAPO has never been challenged either from within the party or outside it and he recently completed his third term as president by popular acclaim, notwithstanding that this required the passing of a constitutional amendment in 2003–4. In South Africa, the mantle of Nelson Mandela has passed to Thabo Mbeki, even if he is unable to exert the same charisma as his illustrious predecessor. Nevertheless, he has held the ANC together since his accession to power in 1999 and enlarged its support base. In 1995, there were many who anticipated that the ANC would fragment after the elections due in 1999. That did not happen either then or in 2004 and currently there seems little that will seriously challenge the ANC's dominance in government. Chief Gatsha Buthelezi, however strong he may still be in KwaZulu Natal, has not in recent years seriously attempted to challenge the ANC at national level. He remains a regional rather than a national political leader, a status reinforced in 2004 when he lost his place in Mbeki's cabinet as minister of home affairs.

Secondly, linked with the importance of political personalities, is the size of government majorities. This has been very marked in South Africa and Namibia since their accession to majority rule in 1994 and 1990 respectively. After the merging of ZANU and ZAPU in Zimbabwe in 1988, the government of Robert Mugabe faced an exiguous parliamentary opposition for most of the 1990s,[52] and this only changed with the formation of Morgan Tsvangirai's MDC in 1997 when Mugabe came to face an opposition only a few seats short of those occupied by ZANU-PF. It was perhaps this accretion of power to the MDC that prompted Mugabe to behave as he did for fear of losing his political dominance. While in Swaziland parliamentary majorities are not relevant because of the nature of the political system, in Botswana the BDP under Presidents Khama, Masire and currently Mogae has always enjoyed a substantial majority over all other parties and this has enabled it to govern with greater quietude than might otherwise have been the case. This has been buttressed by the government's respect for constitutionality and 'due process', making it – along with South Africa – one of the most transparent governments on the African continent. Unfortunately, this has not applied in Lesotho, where political leaders, both civil and military, have at intervals forsaken the strict path of constitutionality and endeavoured to gain their objectives through *ultra vires* acts of the kind already referred to.

Thirdly, and as a direct corollary of the size of governing majorities, political oppositions tend to be weak and fragmented, even if tolerated. In South Africa in 2004, the election was contested by 21 parties: of these, seven gained parliamentary representation, the ANC achieving 279 seats and a majority of 178 over all other parties. The Democratic Alliance, with 50 seats, was its closest rival followed by the Inkatha Freedom Party with 28; the United Democratic Movement, the New National Party, the Pan-African Congress and the Freedom Front polled 23 between them. There were few, if any, common political denominators between these parties and consequently little prospect of any united or coherent opposition to the ANC. In this situation, the latter is likely to become comatose and complacent in terms of policy formulation and political originality. Similar situations prevail in Botswana and Namibia where governing majority parties are large and constructive challenge to their policies correspondingly weak. Indeed opposition to government policies in both countries comes mainly from the media, which may account for the fact that in Namibia journalists have in recent years come in for a certain amount of pressure from government which can in no way be described as proper.[53] Botswana, however, has a clean record in this respect.

Fourthly, there are the issues of transparency, freedom from corruption and the 'democratic spirit' and, over these, generalisation is far from easy. Zimbabwe under its present regime fails the test on every count with its manipulation of food aid, its treatment of its political opponents, its attacks on both the judiciary and the media and its alleged complicity in election-rigging, and it would appear that these will only cease when and if the regime falls. Angola, whilst it is rapidly consolidating after the trauma of its long civil war, still has much ground to make up in terms of improving its regional administration and increasing its financial transparency over the collection of and accounting for oil revenues. Mozambique has succeeded against the odds in securing the active participation of RENAMO in the civil development of the state and its increasingly pluralistic nature, even if many of its citizens still equate successful democracy with growing economic prosperity and declining unemployment rather than due process, respect for minority rights and adherence to the rule of law. Namibia behaves properly in the parliamentary arena but is less tolerant of the mass media when they criticise government policy. Swaziland has to endure the whims of monarchical absolutism, which has not been present in the UK since Stuart or even Tudor times and how long it will be willing to endure these with equanimity remains a matter of conjecture. In South Africa, Botswana and, to a rather lesser extent, Lesotho, there is evidence of a predilection for more openness and transparency in government than exists in other parts of the region. Lesotho's arraignment of those responsible for financial malpractice in the Lesotho Highlands Water Project,[54] and South Africa's of former deputy president Jacob Zuma on fraud and corruption charges are encouraging pointers for the future. President Mbeki, to his credit and notwithstanding his personal friendship with his deputy, did not feel he could disregard the unfavourable comments made about Zuma by the judge at the trial of Schabir Shaik in June 2005 and dismissed him as deputy president forthwith. Mbeki's action is likely to send a salutary message to the upper echelons of the ANC that standards of conduct in public life must be beyond reproach: indeed, it sends such a message to all the governments of Southern Africa.[55] This may prove to be Mbeki's principal contribution to public administration in the region generally.

# 3   The security dimension

In the Southern Africa of the colonial period, all but the most purblind of the White settlers appreciated the underlying weakness of their situation when set against the size and potential strength of the African majority. In South Africa, there was one White for every five non-Whites, in Rhodesia one for 24 and in Portuguese Africa one for 40. The determination of all the governments in Southern Africa and in Lisbon to maintain White rule for the indefinite future meant that the security dimension was one which had to be considered with the greatest of care, since failure to keep the hatches firmly battened down was likely to have dire consequences for the survival of White minority rule. This chapter, therefore, will concern itself, initially, with the ways in which the Whites maintained control and, later, with the methods employed by the independent governments to ensure the maintenance of order in the new states over which they presided. This search for security is indeed likely to dominate the future of Southern Africa as much as it has dominated that of its past.

Crucial, however, to an understanding of White political thought in Southern Africa generally is the concept of the 'laager mentality'. The overwhelming majority of Whites both in and out of government had a mindset whereby they saw Blacks as constituting a collective threat to their political hegemony, to their economic well-being and indeed to their whole way of life. The danger lay partly in their proximity and partly in their numbers: to avert this, it was necessary to control their behaviour, their work activity, their locus of residence and their education. Provided this was done with sufficient rigour, it would be perfectly possible for Whites, or so they believed, not merely to survive in Southern Africa but also to prosper. Survival and prosperity, however, could never be taken for granted; the White guard would always need to be maintained and the African constantly made to know his place and, whenever necessary, kept in it. One should perhaps recall the words of

Dr Albert Schweitzer of Lambarene when speaking of the European's relations with the African: 'Yes, I am your brother, it is true. But your elder brother.' This general sentiment – and much less benign versions of it – tended to characterise the attitude of Europeans in their dealings with Africans. It was a sentiment from which, over time, much ill was to flow, for Africans were thereby made to feel chronically inferior in the land of their birth.

In Portuguese Africa, security was maintained by a rigorous system of labour control over all non-assimilated Africans, mention of which has already been made.[1] The requirement upon them to work a six-month contract for a European employer had three interlocking advantages: it provided the colonial authority and the White settlers with an assured labour supply, it helped to keep Africans out of mischief and it enhanced their general existence by teaching them 'the ennobling virtue of work'. The fact that their lives were to a greater or lesser extent controlled by the authority of Lisbon meant that the latter's task in maintaining general security was much easier. Lisbon pointed out the path that Africans were to follow and for many years the overwhelming majority did what was expected of them. Their labour contracts over, they returned to their subsistence farms and scratched what they could from their small and uneconomic plots of land until their next contract was due. Whilst this was 'work', it was not of the 'ennobling' kind envisaged by the Portuguese.

It was, however, the forced-labour system (*chibalo*) which was the prime cause of African oppression and resentment.[2] Every so often local administrators would swoop without warning on unsuspecting Africans if labour were required for one public works project or another. These might range from the building of dirt roads through the bush to urban street cleaning and sewer maintenance. In extreme cases, when recruits were required for the police or army, the military police would press-gang Africans of military age on the open road or in their villages. Notwithstanding their tears and protests and without their being able to say their farewells to friends and family, these unfortunate young men would find themselves whisked off to another part of the country and sometimes even to another country altogether to serve in this capacity.[3]

It is, therefore, not surprising that, over time, the colonial rule of Portugal became bitterly unpopular. Salazar's 'New State' policy, which came into force early in the 1930s and which was intentionally modelled on Mussolini's policy for his Italian colonies, imposed a highly disciplinarian system on Angola, Mozambique and Portuguese Guinea. Salazar's colonial policy did not subscribe to the political freedom which, by the early 1960s, the wind of change was bringing to much of

the continent. Indeed Salazar set a determined face against any conces-
sion to this wind of change. This intransigence prompted the outbreak
of wars of liberation in 1961. These broke out in all three of Portugal's
imperial territories, wars of attrition which were to continue until 1974
and which were brought to an end only by the revolt of the Army and
the subsequent announcement by the new government that Portugal
was abandoning its African empire.[4]

Southern Rhodesia, part of the Central African Federation until 1963,
reverted to its original name of 'Rhodesia' on the break-up of the federation in that year. Southern Rhodesia sought independence for itself
along with Northern Rhodesia and Nyasaland at that time, but this
was refused by the London government on the ground that majority
rule did not pertain there.[5] In security terms, the situation for Africans
was broadly similar to that of Portuguese Africa, though there was
no demand for forced labour. In the main towns passes had to be kept
and shown to White officials on request, for, unless they were actively
contributing to the White economy, Africans were not supposed to be
there. If they were in domestic service, they could sleep on their employers' premises, but their living quarters could not be closer than a certain
distance to the principal residence. Whilst European–African relationships were often quite cordial on the personal, domestic level, the same
could not be said of those at the official level, with any infringements of
the law, however trivial or inadvertent, being treated with considerable
severity. The 'laager mentality' permeated the implementation of the
law: the European needed the labour of the African but did not want his
social presence, believing that any derogation from this principle would
assuredly redound to the Europeans' disadvantage in the end. Thus the
powers of the police and other public officials, though laid down by law,
were less circumscribed and less specific than those which might apply
in the United States or Western Europe. Statutes limiting the freedom
of the person – the Unlawful Organisations, the Preventive Detention
and the Law and Order (Maintenance) Acts being the main examples
of this – were in place by the end of the 1950s, long before the demise
of the Central African Federation. During its last two years, 1,220 Africans but only two Europeans were prosecuted under these Acts.[6]

The demise of the federation and the subsequent refusal of the
London government to grant Rhodesia the independence which it
had granted to Zambia and Malawi made the White community more
bitter and more defensive. The failure of the Rhodesian Front government of Winston Field in Salisbury to secure independence resulted in
a sharp decline in its popularity and Rhodesian politics shifted a step
further to the right with the unseating of Field as premier by Ian Smith

in the spring of 1964. Smith made further attempts with both the Conservative and Labour governments of Sir Alec Douglas-Home and Harold Wilson respectively to negotiate independence on the basis of continuing minority rule, but the latter, appreciating the antipathy of Commonwealth opinion to such a course of action, refused to compromise. Eventually, in November 1965, Smith judging correctly that the Wilson government could not and would not resist him, did what his immediate predecessor had shrunk from doing and announced Rhodesia's independence unilaterally and illegally. Simultaneously, a state of emergency was declared throughout the country which was to remain in force until the end of the 1970s.

During this long period of emergency rule, due process of law was suspended and devices such as *habeas corpus* became a thing of the past. Many people, both White and African, were taken into custody at the discretion of Smith's security service and held for substantial periods of time without charge or trial, Judith Todd, the daughter of the former prime minister Garfield Todd, amongst them. Garfield Todd himself had to endure four years of house arrest for his criticisms of the Smith government. Indeed it would hardly be an exaggeration to say that the kind of security system established by Smith and his cabinet after UDI would not have been out of place in the contemporaneous authoritarian regimes of the right – Franco's Spain or Salazar's Portugal and, just slightly later, the Greece of the colonels. Only by these punitive measures, it was adjudged in Salisbury, could the White laager be sufficiently fortified to ensure the survival of 'Christianity and civilised standards' far into the future.

Notwithstanding the mounting of mandatory economic sanctions by the UN Security Council and the refusal of any country, including Portugal and South Africa, to recognise the legitimacy of the Smith regime, the latter survived for more than a decade after UDI. This was largely due to the refusal of both Portugal and South Africa to cooperate on the issue of economic sanctions: irksome though both these states found UDI in the sense that it raised the political temperature in the region very considerably, it was in the interest of neither to see a successful UN campaign mounted against Rhodesia, for this would not only weaken the White laager but also raise the possibility of a similar campaign being mounted against themselves.

Early in 1970 Smith felt strong enough to declare Rhodesia a republic, thus severing her last link with the Crown. Both Britain and the international community had entirely failed in their endeavours to bring the illegal regime to heel and Smith, by virtue of this declaration, poured salt into the wounds he had inflicted five years previously. It evinced the determination of the White community to go its own way and strengthen the laager quite irrespective of either British or international opinion. It might then have been argued that Rhodesia would have gone on to develop a pattern of White hegemony similar to that of South Africa. That this did not happen was due to the collapse, just four years later, of Portuguese colonial power in Mozambique and Angola, which transformed the strategic situation in Southern Africa in a way which none of the principal regional actors could have foreseen and, more specifically, opened up the northern and eastern borders of Rhodesia to guerrilla activity by Rhodesia's African nationalists. The period 1974–9 saw an ever increasing growth in this activity and a corresponding mobilisation of the White settler community to combat it. The young and even the middle-aged were subjected to conscription for three to four months every year to fight in a bush war against ZANU guerrilla bands operating out of Mozambique with the support of its new African government, FRELIMO (the Front for the Liberation of Occupied Mozambique). Rhodesia's Whites had not reckoned with this eventuality, most were not fitted for military service of this kind and certainly very few liked it. Many took one-way tickets to South Africa and this resulted in a drain of men of military age which was eventually to prove fatal to the forcible maintenance of White rule. This, combined with continuing economic sanctions by Britain and the international community and diminishing support from South Africa for Rhodesia's eternally defiant political stance, finally brought Smith to the realisation that the power he held in his hand had become a Dead Sea fruit. In 1979, he was finally persuaded to return to negotiations with the British government. The outcome, following discussions at Lancaster House between Smith, the British government, Nkomo and Mugabe, was the renunciation of UDI, the appointment of a British governor to oversee the transition process to majority rule (which included free elections based on full adult franchise) and, finally, the creation of the new state of Zimbabwe in April 1980.

In South Africa, the Nationalists' victory in the general election of 1948 ushered in the era of apartheid. It represented the determination of the White community to strengthen the laager by policies of racial differentiation in every sphere of human activity. As in Rhodesia, the laws over the freedom of the person tended to reflect this and gave very considerable discretion to individual police officers as to just how – and how far – they should be implemented. Under the Suppression of Communism Act of 1950 membership of a communist party became a criminal offence but matters did not rest there. In subsequent years, people were indicted under this act for uttering views which might be construed as socialist in nature or critical of the country's apartheid system. To its credit, the South African judiciary took as apolitical a view of cases coming before it as circumstances permitted and not infrequently acquitted those arraigned under it, but this law remained a weapon in the hands of the executive in its pursuit of those who held unpalatable views or views which could be portrayed as potentially subversive. This law was not used against the generality of Africans but rather against journalists who wrote and spoke their minds and indeed anyone who might broadly be described as operating within the political arena. Although successful police prosecutions under this act were by no means guaranteed, it did, without question, discourage the candid expression of opinion which in Western Europe and the USA would have been taken entirely for granted.

This act was amended and made more draconian in 1976 when it was renamed the Internal Security Act.[7] Under it, the government obtained the power to ban newspapers which in its view promoted communist ideals or endangered public security and the rightness of its view could not be challenged in the courts. Fourteen Black journalists were detained under it for unfavourably reporting police–demonstrator clashes in Soweto in 1976. The Terrorism Act of 1967 was even more loosely defined: it became an offence to publish material which conduced people towards terrorism without clearly defining the scope of the term. The act thereby gave more or less carte blanche to police officers to detain anyone for a public-order offence, of the terroristic nature of which they would be sole judge: indeed, it was often debatable whether any offence at all had been committed. What was perhaps most objectionable about this act was that people could be held indefinitely without charge or trial and often in solitary confinement. Police, moreover, had power to ban access for people so detained to both lawyers and doctors, which constituted a gross derogation from the freedom of the person. Indeed, with this and similar legislation, there was in fact no freedom.

This freedom, or rather lack of it, extended also to the intellect. The Publications and Entertainments Act of 1963 and later the Publications Act of 1974 empowered the police to search for 'undesirable literature', seize it and submit it to a government committee, the Publications Control Board, which would then determine whether or not it was fit for public consumption. Again, neither act laid down in definitive terms what constituted 'undesirable' and authors inevitably became wary of giving rein to originality lest they be denied publication. Laws of this kind inevitably stultified the development of South African literature throughout the apartheid era: by 1974, even the works of such prominent Afrikaner writers as André Brink and Breyten Breytenbach had been banned.[8]

This legislation was pernicious less for what it did (bad though this was) than for the tone it set. So vague was the wording of much of the security legislation that police officers and other officials charged with enforcing the law felt that they could interpret it more or less as they pleased and that they would not have to account for their actions before any court of law. Challenging police decisions was moreover often not possible because the legislation had excluded the courts from enquiring into the rationale of executive acts. Thus after 1948, South Africa developed into a tyranny, a situation made the more insidious because it occurred against a backdrop of democracy, constitutionality and respect for the rights of the individual against the state. Sadly, that backdrop was no more than a façade, behind which much was happening to rot the South African state. The establishment in 1969 of the Bureau of State Security (BOSS) by Prime Minister Vorster and responsible only to him represented a watershed in the development of the sophisticated police state South Africa had by then become, for BOSS activities were likewise excluded from both parliamentary and judicial scrutiny.

Since the fall of apartheid in 1990, 'security' has become increasingly multi-faceted. The term encompasses many phenomena often only indirectly connected to one another but, taken as a whole, immensely important to the safety in both body and goods enjoyed by ordinary people. Such diseases as AIDS, the lack of stable employment for many, the insouciant behaviour in all too many instances of men towards their womenfolk, continuing inequality in land-ownership across the racial divide and, at a higher level, a reluctance by many to use their political rights to the full all derogate from Southern Africa's 'security' in some measure. This section of the chapter, however, will focus on the concept's more traditional aspects – domestic crime and the policing thereof, illegal immigration, the spill-over of civil conflict into neighbouring states' border areas, gun-running and drug-running across frontiers. However acquisitive by nature man may be, it is almost certainly the case that the cycle of poverty and deprivation so characteristic of the region greatly exacerbates the extent to which people need to resort to illegal activity, great or small, in order to make ends meet. For example, crossing the Mozambique–South Africa border without proper authority or identification papers is a crime, but perhaps a venial one when prompted by people's hope of a better life in a country other than their own.

Firstly, then, illegal immigration. This is a problem primarily affecting the Republic of South Africa as 'lead goose', in economic terms, of the Southern African Development Community. South Africa, even in apartheid days, attracted migrant labour from its neighbours immediately to the north, the discriminatory racial politics of the period notwithstanding: many, if not most, were able to enter legally because Pretoria needed their labour for its gold and diamond mines, and over the years a regular and mutually advantageous migrant labour system was established. Whilst apartheid's demise in the early 1990s did not spell the end of that requirement, the dislocation caused by civil wars in both Angola and Mozambique did lead to greatly enhanced demand from would-be immigrants on South African 'hospitality'. However parlous the socio-economic situation might be for the generality of South Africans, it was seen as a new Jerusalem by Angolans, Namibians, Mozambicans and Zimbabweans who were, by 1995, crossing the frontier, mostly illegally, at the rate of 200,000 per month because of the lack of employment opportunities in their own countries.[9] Some were electrocuted trying to cross the wire fences at the frontier, others were devoured by wild animals attempting to cross the Kruger National Park, but most got through and their determination to do so was an attestation of both their courage and the desperate socio-economic situation in their own countries. Once in South Africa, if they did not get apprehended for illegal entry and sent back across the frontier, they might be employed in South African concerns (generally farms) at starvation wages which, rather than make a fuss, they would accept for fear of drawing attention to their illegal status. This practice had the effect of lowering wages generally, but especially in the frontier areas, and tended to make the illegal migrants extremely unpopular with indigenous Black South Africans infuriated at seeing their own level of wages thus depressed. Many problems of communication resulted in the schools also as, generally speaking, the children of these new migrants were unable to speak the same language as the children of the indigenous inhabitants, and neither were their teachers. This problem has now been extant for over a decade and shows little sign of abating. One of two things will have to happen before it does so – either more economic development will have to occur in countries to South Africa's north to discourage the southward drift of population or else South Africa's own economy must expand sufficiently to accommodate this influx. Neither is perhaps very likely, but the first possibility would be much more desirable than the second: it falls to South Africa, through SADC, to encourage a more even spread of economic development throughout the region.

Secondly, crime – especially violent crime. During the apartheid period, a certain cult of violence grew up and came to be widely accepted. For Whites, violence was necessary to defend 'the laager'; for Blacks and other non-Whites, it was essential for encompassing its overthrow. Nelson Mandela in 1962 spoke openly of the inevitability of and need for violence and spent the next 27 years in prison as a result. Though the

ANC engaged in violent acts from time to time, both the ordinary and state security police deployed it on a regular – and vicious – basis as a matter of course. Sadly, the demise of apartheid in the early 1990s did not result in the abandonment of this cult. On 6 September 1996, South Africa's *Financial Mail* carried out an opinion poll on the country's principal problems, which indicated that 45 per cent of the population regarded crimes of violence as the most urgent issue followed by unemployment at only 18 per cent. Lack of decent housing and sub-standard education attracted 4 per cent and 2 per cent of the vote respectively. These are startling figures but readily explicable in terms of crime statistics. In an Interpol report of 1995–6, South Africa was found to have 53.4 murders per 100,000 head of population[10] and 99.7 rapes; of these, less than half came to trial and convictions resulted in 11 per cent and 8 per cent of cases.

There are a number of reasons for this sorry record. Firstly, the political changes of 1994 demanded that the police take a distinctly more lenient approach to offenders. This came to be exploited by offenders and the police were left confused and demoralised at the need to vary their previous 'strong-arm' approach: indeed, they were not infrequently accused by the public of pussyfooting. Secondly, the massive growth of the private security industry since 1990–1 has blurred the *raison d'être* of the ordinary police and indeed attracted them into the private sector where the rates of pay are higher. Thirdly, the police are chronically overborne by the sheer level of crime, both violent and non-violent: South Africa heads the world league for murder and is eleventh in that league for aggravated assault. It is hardly surprising, therefore, that those who can afford it (mainly middle-class Whites) subscribe to private firms to protect their properties and that much 'siege architecture', namely high walls, alarm systems and barbed wire, adorns the suburbs of South Africa's major cities. Naturally, wealthy Whites present tempting targets for impoverished non-Whites, but these latter, most of whom are perfectly law-abiding, in no way enjoy similar protection from the ordinary police as Whites do from their private security firms, the staff of which outnumber the police by the order of two to one. In consequence, much 'Black-on-Black' violence goes unremedied – and unreported – reflecting the situation of the apartheid era when most of the resources of the police were devoted to protecting the White community.[11]

The security of states is also affected by events beyond their borders, most notably by civil wars, but also by civil commotion and organised crime. This was particularly the case in Namibia during the 1990s when its most northerly province of Ovamboland was severely disrupted by the civil war between the MPLA and UNITA in their struggle to control

Angola. The borders were frequently violated when one party was in military 'hot pursuit' of the other and there was much damage to the border fencing. These incursions had the effect of terrorising (and terrifying) the local population and had a severely adverse effect on Ovamboland's economy. Even though the relationship between the two governments was basically amicable, the failure of the MPLA government of Angola to control these incursions made at times for strained relations with Namibia which had to 'pick up the pieces' in a conflict not its own.

Likewise, at about the same time, the civil war in Mozambique between FRELIMO and RENAMO 'spilled over' into Swaziland, with frequent border violations and much drug- and gun-running occurring in Mozambique under the cover of civil war and a lucrative trade in stolen cars. All this illegal activity greatly upset the local Swazi population, especially those resident in the border areas, but there was relatively little by way of remedial action that the royal government could take regarding it – other than make formal protests to Maputo. Indeed the latter, itself struggling with a civil war, was overborne in attempting to control this criminal activity and this was eventually accepted by the Swazi government, the adverse consequences for its own population notwithstanding. What needs to be emphasised is that an upheaval in any one country can have repercussions well beyond that country's borders. The civil wars in both Angola and Mozambique triggered off events which not only affected Namibia and Swaziland but also South Africa, in that the latter had to combat both illegal arms- and drug-trafficking, which these conflicts had occasioned, and crime in South Africa was much augmented thereby.

Though crime has been a serious and growing problem throughout Southern Africa in recent years, it is perhaps in South Africa itself that it has been most manifest – and most vicious. Reference has already been made to the crime statistics, those for murder and other forms of violence being distressingly high. The spillover of external conflicts and the headlong rush southwards of illegal migrants have both contributed to this, but more fundamental features of the new South African polity have also played their part. Firstly, South Africa is the most populous and prosperous state in the Southern African constellation; as such, it attracts the criminal element as well as those legitimately seeking work. Secondly, its borders are porous and impossible to police thoroughly: it has, for example, 52 international crossing points compared with Zimbabwe's seven.[12] Thirdly, its transportation and banking infrastructure are by regional standards sophisticated and contribute enormously to the economic development of the country, but they also facilitate the speed at which criminals can move from one place to another and the extent to which money dishonestly gained can be rapidly laundered; it is probably no exaggeration to say that the police are at present quite unable to contain this spread of crime in all its various manifestations. This is particularly serious when viewed against the decline in police morale which has occurred since 1994. G. Arnold, R.I. Rotberg and G. Mills have all made invaluable appraisals of the security situation in South Africa in the works referenced.

There are further kinds of crime which, whilst not unique to South Africa, are certainly very prominent there. One is drug-running, which has become endemic since 1980, in such substances as heroin, cocaine and mandrax (an artificially produced sedative made from antihistamines and methaqualone powder). This traffic has been fomented and exploited over the years by foreign elements, particularly Nigerians, who have inveigled their way into the country as tourists and subsequently succeeded by devious means in obtaining South African passports. The dominance of Nigeria's position in this trade is illustrated by the fact that in 1993, more than half of the cocaine smuggled into South Africa was found in the possession of Nigerian nationals and in the following year, 1994, 30 per cent of all the heroin seized at points of entry in the USA was in the same hands.[13] The drug scene has become a serious problem for South Africa, in that the traffickers now regard it as a good market in itself, not merely as a good conduit country for the exporting of drugs elsewhere as was originally the case in the early 1990s. The impact of this traffic on crime generally in South Africa can only be guessed at. Certainly, the South African government was sufficiently alarmed by the extent of the problem to host a joint EU–SADC conference in 1995 in an attempt to address it at a high strategic level through a process of intelligence-gathering and institution-building (anti-corruption laws, protection of judiciaries from intimidation, conspiracy investigation policies) across frontiers.

Another problem is vehicle theft, sometimes known as carjacking. This is not just ordinary car-stealing, but theft of a vehicle in which an element of violence is involved, when it enters or leaves a parking lot, or when it is halted at traffic lights. The driver's window is smashed with the butt of a firearm and the driver intimidated into leaving his vehicle. This is then driven away into a remote part of the city and, within hours, it is stripped down and its registration plates are changed and chassis numbers filed away, and it is given an altogether new identity which makes it subsequently very difficult for the police to trace or recognise. Surveillance by police and army helicopters have made some progress in addressing this problem, though it remains nevertheless a considerable thorn in the side of the police – and of the public.

All these various phenomena – violent crime, spillover of conflict into neighbouring states, the relentless southward push of poverty-stricken people, drug- and gun-running, inadequate public policing – contribute to the insecurity which characterises the lives of so many in Southern Africa. So too does a socio-economic situation of great disparity and uncertainty and the ever-present threat of physical illness, notably AIDS, which has been ravaging the region since the early 1990s. On some fronts, governments can show leadership by endeavouring to change attitudes and culture: they must ensure, for example, that the state and the state alone enjoys a monopoly of coercive power. On others, it is probably only the onward march of education that will eventually bring about greater enlightenment, greater tolerance and the greatest happiness of the greatest number throughout Southern Africa.

# 4 The foreign policy dimension

Of the countries of Southern Africa in the late 1940s, only the Union of South Africa (as it then was) could be described as having its own foreign policy. All the others were in different ways dependent or colonial territories: Namibia continued to be regarded by South Africa as a League of Nations mandate; Great Britain was responsible for Southern Rhodesia's foreign policy under the terms of the 1923 settlement as well as for the protectorates of Northern Rhodesia and Nyasaland. Angola and Mozambique, being colonies of Portugal, had by definition no foreign policy of their own. To the extent that it mattered at all, foreign policy was determined in faraway capitals – London, Lisbon or Pretoria as the case might be. Not for many years after 1948 did foreign policy either relating to Southern Africa or emanating from it become a matter of great import.

South Africa, then as now, dominated the region in terms of both political experience and economic muscle. Its mineral resources were massive and much in demand in international markets. It had graduated from membership of the British Empire to statehood in 1910 and remained a member of the British Commonwealth of Nations for many years thereafter. Notwithstanding the narrowness of its political base and electoral franchise, it had participated with honour in both world wars, emerging on both occasions on the winning side and achieving, thereby, an aura of international respectability in the Western world. For the Soviet Union, South Africa was at the other end of a continent which was itself remote and its capitalist system, though unwelcome, was not something about which much could be done. Outside the world of the West, the continents of Asia and Africa remained for the most part under colonial rule, the one exception being the Indian subcontinent, which became independent in the period 1947–8. Faced with the manifold problems of independence, these states had little time to concern themselves with foreign policy in general or with South Africa in particular.

This, besides, was before the apartheid era and South Africa, notwithstanding the discrimination on grounds of race which existed even then in many spheres of life, was not overtly a racist state. It was presided over by Field Marshal Jan Smuts of the United Party, a man of the utmost international respectability, a member of the British war cabinet in both world wars and instrumental in the defeat of both German and Japanese fascism. However, in the general election of May 1948, Smuts and his United Party were defeated, albeit narrowly, by the National Party of D.F. Malan on a manifesto which wrote racial differentiation into the law of the land and set in train the apartheid era.[1]

Pervasive and cruel though the apartheid legislation passed in succeeding years was, it never attracted as much unfavourable international comment – at any rate for much of the 1950s – as might have been supposed. However, two interconnected events combined to bring about a very different situation by the end of that decade. The first was a general loosening of Europe's imperial grip on her various territories which had already started in the 1940s with the British decolonisation of the Indian subcontinent, the retreat of the Dutch from Indonesia and the challenge to the French position in Indo-China. The second was the unsuccessful Anglo-French military intervention in Egypt in November 1956 to regain control of the Suez Canal, nationalised by President Nasser the previous July. His successful defiance of Britain and France at that time appeared to signal to the colonised world that colonialism was on the run. Criticism of the Franco-British intervention at Suez in both UN and Commonwealth circles was almost universal, Jawaharlal Nehru of India being particularly supportive of Egypt and condemnatory of British and French neo-colonialism. More significantly, France and Britain failed to secure American diplomatic support for their intervention: Washington threatened to withdraw its support from both the pound and the franc in the world's money markets and the voting at the UN General Assembly at this time demonstrated as clearly as anything the extent to which Britain and France were isolated on this issue.[2]

So, by the end of the 1950s, the Third World and the 'new' Commonwealth within it were on the march. The latter was important in the sense that it spanned two continents, Asia and Africa, enabling it to represent itself as expressing the opinion of both. By this time, there was much criticism in Commonwealth circles of South Africa's policy of apartheid, though from the newer rather than the older members. South Africa's wish to remain a member of the Commonwealth after becoming a republic in the early 1960s did not find general favour. Commonwealth rules stipulated that any country wanting to become a republic had to re-apply for membership. In most cases, this was purely a formality, but not so in that of South Africa. Even before Tanganyika became independent in 1961, its nationalist leader Julius Nyerere let it be known that he would be unhappy about his country continuing as a member of the Commonwealth if South Africa were permitted to rejoin as a republic. He was supported in this sentiment by Nehru of India, as well as a number of fellow African nationalists. As a result of this diplomatic commotion, South Africa, being unwilling to compromise on the principle of apartheid, decided not to apply for renewal of its Commonwealth membership after becoming a republic. Thus was the issue defused, but the unacceptability of apartheid in Commonwealth politics had become plain for all to see. Majority, not minority, rule was what was now demanded.

Nowhere was this seen more starkly than at the time of Rhodesia's unilateral declaration of independence (UDI) in November 1965. Rhodesia had tried, and failed, to persuade Britain to grant her independence on the basis of minority rule. UDI was her attempt to take unconstitutionally what she had been constitutionally denied. Britain knew by 1965 that to grant Rhodesia independence on any basis, other than one of African majority rule, would split the Commonwealth and lead thereby to its demise, an outcome she could not contemplate politically. Nor, with only the narrowest of parliamentary majorities, could Harold Wilson's government contemplate the use of force to bring Ian Smith's Rhodesian Front government to heel. The result was that, whilst the Commonwealth survived, Britain's reputation within it, due to its failure to stand up for the political rights of Rhodesia's African population, fell to a level not seen since the Suez Crisis of 1956.

If UDI was embarrassing for London, it was almost equally so for Pretoria. Pretoria did not wish to exacerbate its relations with London nor to see the searchlight of international opinion beamed onto the racial problems of Southern Africa, but equally White public opinion would not countenance the undermining of the Smith regime which cooperation with UN sanctions would unquestionably entail. Pretoria, therefore, had to rally, however unwillingly, in defence of the White laager. It had to allow Rhodesian tobacco exports to get out and imports destined for Rhodesia to get in and could pay but scant regard to either British or international opinion on this issue. It would, by far, have preferred the latter not to have been raised at all, for it cast a most unfavourable light on her own racial policies; besides, a successful economic sanctions campaign against Rhodesia would almost certainly lead, in the next breath, to a similar campaign being mounted against South Africa itself. The Smith regime, too, was popular amongst White South Africans who saw him as standing for the same ideals as themselves. Were they not all, indeed, defending White rule in the southern part of the continent? So the then prime minister, H. Verwoerd, announced a policy of 'business as usual', as indeed did Salazar in Lisbon. This meant no participation in UN sanctions but, equally, no recognition of Ian Smith's illegal regime. Indeed, no country on the face of the earth accorded it recognition in diplomatic terms, though in economic and commercial terms many maintained a policy of 'business as usual'.[3] The refusal of both South Africa and Portugal to cooperate on the sanctions issue meant that Wilson's aim of bringing the Smith regime to its knees 'within weeks rather than months' was thwarted. The regime, despite being unrecognised, survived – much to the humiliation of Britain and to the exasperation of the newly independent states of Africa and of others in the Third World.

In an attempt to lower the hostile political pressure thereby generated, South Africa embarked in the late 1960s on an 'outward-looking' foreign policy towards its neighbours further north. This policy encompassed a non-confrontational approach by Pretoria to many, if not all of the independent states of West, Central and East Africa. It involved continuing dialogue and promises of economic and technical aid in exchange for not pressing South Africa on the apartheid issue. The more radical of the African states refused to have anything to do with Pretoria's blandishments – Tanzania, Zambia and Guinea to name just three. Many, however, did – Nigeria, Ghana, Kenya, Ivory Coast and Zaire amongst them. Perhaps most remarkable of all was the rapport that developed between Malawi and South Africa: Malawi, being intensely poor in both natural and human resources, saw entering a close economic and commercial relationship with South Africa as its best way forward and, to achieve this, was prepared to suppress its objections to South Africa's policies on the political level. President Hastings Banda was rewarded for his cooperation with an invitation to make a state visit to South Africa in October 1971, at that time the first African head of state ever to be accorded this honour. Whilst this did nothing to endear Dr Banda to some of his immediate neighbours or to the Organisation of African Unity, it certainly served to give Malawi much-needed economic and technical aid. Malawi's new capital city of Lilongwe was largely built therefore with South African capital and technical expertise. The message from South Africa to the independent states of Central Africa was essentially this: 'curtail your criticisms of us on the political front and we will ensure that your problems on the economic front are eased as much as possible'.

This policy was initiated in 1966 under the Vorster administration and was the brainchild of his foreign minister, 'Pik' Botha. It was only very partially successful at diminishing the resentment of Africa's independent states at Rhodesia's UDI and South Africa's own racial policies, but it did mitigate the active opposition which might otherwise have come from these states. This policy remained extant until the middle of the 1970s, when the collapse of Portugal's imperial position in Southern Africa raised African expectation of significant political change and put South Africa itself on the strategic defensive vis-à-vis its immediate neighbours in a way it had not experienced before.

This change of situation had come about remarkably rapidly. In 1973 politicians looking north from Pretoria would have seen no particular signs of strategic alarm. Within two years, however, South Africa had succeeded in getting itself involved in the civil war of national liberation which occurred in Angola in the wake of Portugal's withdrawal. Its support for UNITA, the southernmost of the three nationalist movements and anti-Marxist, could not prevail against the MPLA, which was massively supported by the Soviet Union and Cuba, and the South African army had to beat an orderly, but undignified, retreat out of Angola back across the Cunene River into Namibia (see Map F, p. 51). Though not a military defeat, it was definitely a psychological one and seen by the Black population of South Africa as a distinct strategic setback for the forces of White supremacy. This perception encouraged mass protests against government policy over primary education in Soweto and other townships, protests which were met by repression. Though Pretoria was successful in containing the situation in the short term, the Black population had tasted blood and, after 1976, was prepared to defy the White establishment in a way it had not done before.

By the time P.W. Botha became prime minister in 1978, South Africa was under pressure from both within and without. Firstly, it had not been able to contain the situation in Angola where the pro-Marxist MPLA had increasingly asserted its authority against UNITA in the country's southern provinces; secondly, Ian Smith in Rhodesia had failed to tame the ZAPU and ZANU nationalist movements who were being helped in this regard by the FRELIMO government of Mozambique. The latter was also offering the African National Congress military training facilities on its territory to wage guerrilla war against the Republic of South Africa. Faced with this situation, Pretoria, whilst maintaining a benign face to those Central African states which had acquiesced in its outward-looking foreign policy in the late 1960s and 1970s, attempted to destabilise those regimes in Southern Africa which it suspected were offering aid and comfort either to the ANC in South Africa or to the South West African People's Organisation (SWAPO) in Namibia. This meant that relations between South African, Angola, Mozambique and, to a lesser extent, Zimbabwe became distinctly frosty and Pretoria did its utmost in the early 1980s to support the RENAMO movement in its struggle against the FRELIMO government in Maputo. It also gave what continued assistance it could to Jonas Savimbi's UNITA movement in southern Angola against the MPLA, partly because of its own ideological hostility to it as a Marxist grouping and partly because of the latter's support of SWAPO, which was doing its utmost to undermine South Africa's position in Namibia. Both Angola and Mozambique had to be neutralised because of their willingness to wage guerrilla war against South Africa and weaken it on every possible front.

All this led to considerable friction between South Africa and her neighbours to the north and proved counterproductive for all parties. In an endeavour to achieve a modus vivendi, South Africa and Mozambique came to an agreement at Nkomati in 1984, whereby South Africa would cease assisting RENAMO against Maputo and Mozambique would withdraw training and other military support facilities on its territory from the ANC in its battle against Pretoria. The truth of the matter was that the principal antagonists were coming under considerable pressure from the proxy forces of the other and needed some respite. The Nkomati Accord did not work too well due to derogations by both sides and was discontinued the following year, though revived again in May 1988 – by which time South Africa was coming under yet greater pressure from the ANC as a result of the upheavals in the townships. The importance of the accord to both countries was evidenced by the fact that Botha paid a state visit to Mozambique in September of that year when he was formally received by President Chissano.

On the other side of the continent, there had been continuous friction between South Africa and Angola ever since the accession to power of the MPLA, following the collapse of Portuguese power in 1974. In 1978, the UN Security Council passed Resolution 435 calling upon South Africa to withdraw from Namibia and allow preparations for majority rule. This South Africa accepted in principle but failed to implement in practice on the ground that Russo-Cuban forces were threatening her security in Namibia by supporting the guerrilla armies of SWAPO in the north of that country, and she was supported in this by the US and the West. For some years, until the accession to power of Gorbachev in the USSR, there was stalemate. However, by 1987, Gorbachev made it clear that the USSR was no longer interested in fighting any kind of Cold War with the West either in Africa or elsewhere and announced the withdrawal of support from his erstwhile allies in both Angola and Namibia. This spelt the end both of the Soviet–Cuban military presence in Angola and of Soviet military support for SWAPO in

Namibia and enabled South Africa, now that it faced no threat from the communist forces north of the Cunene River, to contemplate military disengagement from Namibia. The USA, itself anxious to respond positively to the cooperative spirit of the new Soviet leadership, encouraged Pretoria to do likewise and implement Resolution 435. Over 1988–9 discussions took place between Angola and South Africa on the joint issues of Russo-Cuban disengagement from Angola and of South African withdrawal from Namibia and agreement was reached on this in April 1989, an agreement which also paved the way for the independence of Namibia by way of free elections. Despite the Russo-Cuban military withdrawal from Angola, the loss of Namibia was not an easy pill for Pretoria to swallow. She had had control of the territory since 1919 and regarded it very much as her own demesne. However, by 1989, Pretoria itself was in a state of change, beset by domestic upheaval and economic sanctions from the USA and the European Community (EC).

This had come about as a result of the disturbances in the African townships which the Tricameral Constitution of 1983 had provoked. These were met by the Botha government with repression and the declaration of two states of emergency during the period 1985–6.[4] This involved severe restriction on the press, both domestic and international, as to how events in the townships should be reported or whether indeed they should be reported at all. The policy backfired, because it provoked retaliation from both the USA and the EC in the form of economic sanctions against South African produce with the imposition of embargoes and quotas. A number of private concerns, General Motors and Barclays Bank amongst them, also decided to 'disinvest' from South Africa, given the long-term uncertainty of the political situation. President Reagan's policy of 'constructive engagement' towards South Africa – whereby no sanctions were to be taken but diplomatic suasion used in an attempt to make the Republic more accommodating on the race issue – was effectively overridden by Congress when it rejected two key presidential vetoes on the imposition of economic sanctions. The fact that these were rejected by a two-thirds majority in each house of Congress was reflective of the state of US public opinion at that time, notwithstanding Reagan's personal tendency to be more lenient towards Pretoria. The European Council of Ministers agreed at this same time, without demur, a programme of economic sanctions on South Africa's major agricultural exports in retaliation for her handling of the state of emergency, well described by J. Blumenfeld and his colleagues in *South Africa in Crisis.*[5]

Thus, by the close of the 1980s, South Africa was under siege from both her own Black population in the townships and her allies in the

West. After 1986 she was no longer in a position to make her own foreign policy: her foreign policy thereafter became a matter of reacting to the ebb and flow of events which she could not, in any meaningful sense, control. Her position was eased by the change of regime in the Soviet Union in 1985 and the latter's subsequent retreat from Africa. By 1988–9, the US found itself pushing against a door, in the matter of the decolonisation of Namibia, which, even if not open, was at any rate not locked. American diplomatic demands to South Africa that she should now implement Resolution 435 came to be favourably received, partly because the strategic threat from Angola was clearly vanishing and also because South Africa wanted to mend fences with the USA and the European Community and thereby secure release from the economic sanctions to which she had been subjected. The illness of President Botha early in 1989, his permanent departure from power in the summer of 1989 and his replacement by F.W. de Klerk also eased the transition from a foreign policy of confrontation to one of accommodation. By the end of 1989, South Africa was beginning to come back into the world.

The Republic of South Africa now dominates the foreign policy scene in Southern Africa as Hamlet does the Shakespearean tragedy of the same name. Whilst not always centre stage, its presence is constantly felt and that presence is basically benign, even if, for historical reasons, not always perceived to be so by its neighbours to the north. By virtue of its size, population and economic resources, it is perhaps inevitable that this should be so and it does give that country a role and responsibility in the region to which the other states cannot aspire.

It was not always so: just two decades ago, the situation was very different. The mid- to late 1980s was a period of confrontation between South Africa and its northern neighbours. P.W. Botha ruled in Pretoria and had embarked upon a policy of 'destabilising' those African states north of the Limpopo which were seen to be giving aid and comfort to the ANC: this involved armed incursion into their territories by the most efficient military force on the African continent and could not be easily countered. Considerable destruction of property and loss of innocent life inevitably occurred over a period of three to four years. South Africa's apartheid system seemed invincible and Nelson Mandela languished in Pollsmoor Prison. That this situation changed so quickly, unexpectedly and peacefully at the end of the 1980s and the early 1990s is one of the marvels of our time.

With the accession of Nelson Mandela to the presidency in 1994, South Africa's foreign policy went into complete reverse. There was no longer confrontation but an extension of the hand of friendship and collaboration: Namibia's 700 million rand debt to South Africa, for example, was written off and the port of Walvis Bay, disputed for many years, was handed over to her, something quite inconceivable under the former apartheid regime. Writing in 1993, shortly before he became president, Mandela stated as follows:

> South Africa cannot escape its African destiny. If we do not devote our energies to this continent, we too could fall victim to the forces that have brought ruin to its various parts. Like the United Nations, the Organisation of African Unity needs to be attuned to the changes at work throughout the world . . . Southern Africa commands a special priority in our foreign policy. We are inextricably part of Southern Africa and our destiny is linked to that of a region, which is much more than a mere geographical concept.[6]

Later in that same article, Mandela referred to the importance of establishing South Africa as a sound democracy and one observant of human rights, but essentially he saw Africa as an integral whole and one to whose sound destiny his own country could, by virtue of its own political experience in resolving near intractable disputes, contribute much. He also believed that South Africa had a responsibility to pay back debts to those countries which had assisted the ANC during its struggle of liberation and felt strongly that South Africa's own stability and prosperity could not be advanced in isolation from the rest of the continent. As the wealthiest and most advanced country in Southern Africa, it was only reasonable that South Africa should play a full part in contributing to the continent's development and thereby enhancing its prosperity.[7] This was not merely Mandela's view, but one shared by the G8 and many of the states of Africa. It was thus on a distinctly high note that the new South Africa came into being.

Foreign policy in Southern Africa will now be considered among a number of heads.

### South Africa: Mandela and Mbeki compared and contrasted

Both of South Africa's first two presidents had rather different approaches to foreign policy issues. Nelson Mandela came early to the belief that his country's foreign policy should be based on clear ethical principles and favoured a certain unilateralism which was by no means always appreciated by his counterparts overseas. For example, he fostered close relations with Muammar Gaddafi of Libya, Fidel Castro of Cuba and Deng Xiaoping of the People's Republic of China, all of whom had been supporters of the ANC during the apartheid period –Mandela believed this had to be recognised. However, his attitude greatly irritated Western governments, most notably the administration of US president Bill Clinton. Washington had been applying sanctions against Iran ever since the hostage crisis of November 1979 to January 1981, and against Libya for various alleged acts of terrorism during the 1980s, which culminated in the Lockerbie bombing of 1987, and viewed Mandela's policy as directly contravening this.

Mandela either discounted Western susceptibilities on these matters or else failed to appreciate the depth of Western feeling. Most probably, he was overborne by a sense of gratitude towards these several countries and not therefore prepared to bow to Western diplomatic opinion. He was thus in foreign policy terms very much his own man and the evidence is that he consulted in general rather less than he might have done. An example of this is provided by the execution of Ken Saro-Wiwa and his environmental colleagues from the Ogoni region of Eastern Nigeria in 1995: here, Mandela argued in SADC and Commonwealth fora that sanctions should be taken against the Abacha government and Nigeria expelled from the Commonwealth for abusing Saro-Wiwa's human rights by denying him a trial in open court,[8] ignoring his express plea for clemency and executing him whilst the Commonwealth Heads of Government Meeting (CHOGM) was in session. Though Nigeria was subsequently suspended from the Commonwealth, Mandela's principled stance over Saro-Wiwa did not find favour within SADC, which considered he had exceeded his authority by intervening in what was essentially an internal matter for Nigeria. Naturally, Mandela's reputation in SADC circles suffered and he was gently reminded that South Africa was the last, not the first country in the region to attain its political freedom.

Perhaps partly on account of this, Thabo Mbeki eschewed Mandela's 'ethical approach' to foreign policy when he assumed the presidency in 1999. He was not in any case a man for bold, sweeping gestures, realising all too well that the size and wealth of South Africa rendered her not always entirely popular within Southern Africa's constellation of states. He therefore took pains to work in collaboration with his SADC colleagues on regional issues and to be seen, unlike his illustrious predecessor, as a 'team player'. In this, he has forsaken 'ethics' but concentrated on strengthening South Africa's business links both within and beyond Africa, notably in such countries as China, Brazil and Korea. Perhaps the most notable example of his penchant for collaboration has been the part he played with Olusegen Obasanjo, then president of Nigeria, in getting the New Plan for African Development (NEPAD) under way. (Obasanjo stepped down from power at the

Nigerian presidential election of April 2007 to be succeeded by Umaru Yar'Adua. It is to be hoped that this collaboration will continue in the same vein with Yar'Adua.) This is essentially a long-term plan for the whole African continent which, if successful, will make a notable contribution to its good economic and political governance. It is a venture to which Mbeki has devoted much time during the period of his presidency, to the extent that he has sometimes been criticised in his own country for concentrating too much on this at the expense of domestic policy. It is regrettable that much of the genuine good he has done in this field has been overshadowed by his stance on AIDS and his failure to bring pressure to bear on President Mugabe of Zimbabwe – at any rate in the eyes of the international community.

## The New Plan for African Development (NEPAD) and the African Union (AU)

Though Thabo Mbeki may have differed from Nelson Mandela in his approach to foreign policy, he has espoused with full vigour, since becoming president, Mandela's vision of South Africa becoming a positive and benign force on the continent generally. Writing in *The Sowetan* on 3 October 1997, Mbeki stated as follows:

> The African Renaissance must bring an end to the dictatorships and civil wars that have given Africa the distinction of having the largest number of refugees in the world. We have to address the abuse of national sovereignty where terrible things would be going on within the borders of one country whilst the rest of the continent stands paralysed because taking action could be seen as interference.

To this end, he has made full use of international diplomatic machinery, most notably his chairmanship of the Non-aligned Movement (NAM) and, after becoming president in 1999, exploiting his friendship with Abdulaziz Bouteflika, president of Algeria and also chairman of the Organisation for African Unity (OAU), to devise a timetable on development and debt relief for NEPAD and the OAU to consider. At an Extraordinary OAU Summit in Algiers in June 1999, Bouteflika and Mbeki were given a mandate to advise on the parameters for African economic development and to recommend a 'broad, holistic approach' to achieve it. Out of this, the concept of NEPAD was born and became incorporated into the structure of both the African Union[9] (AU) and SADC in October 2001. The latter was to operate under six portfolios: peace and security, political governance, economic governance, capital flows, human resources and marketing outlets. Standards of performance and stipulations as to 'good practice' were laid down for each of these portfolios and it was the task of the African Peer Group Review Mechanism (APRM) to ensure that these standards and stipulations were met. So far only 12 states have agreed to submit to the APRM, and of these only two SADC states have done so, Mauritius and South Africa. The reports submitted to date have been discussed but not published, which does somewhat reduce their utility. Their aim is to identify weaknesses and devise remedial measures, which will then be rechecked three to five years after the original report.

It is as yet too early to say just how efficiently NEPAD is going to work. The monitoring procedure is cumbersome and takes place in two stages involving considerable delay, and in any case submission to the APRM is voluntary on members. If NEPAD works as envisaged by Presidents Mbeki, Bouteflika and Obasanjo, great good could come of it over time. But it has been opined that NEPAD presupposes a certain degree of regulation and discipline,[10] and whether it can survive upheavals within states and indeed conflicts between states must remain a matter of conjecture. This pessimism is reinforced by the fact that, by 2003, only 12 states had signed up to the peace and security initiative and debates in parliament had taken place in only three of the 25 member states; all this has constituted a distinct disappointment for President Mbeki.

## Peacekeeping missions

There seems to be no end to Africa's wars and there is a bottomless pit for the international community of potential involvement in them. The years since 1993 have seen upheavals in Rwanda, Sierra Leone, Ivory Coast, the Democratic Republic of Congo and, more recently, Sudan. Even tiny Lesotho has had its problems, albeit on a much smaller scale. Bringing peace and stability to Africa is thus a challenge for the UN and, indeed, the continent itself, as most states outside Africa do not see their vital interests affected there and, within Africa, there are probably only two, Nigeria and South Africa, which have the capability to assist in peacekeeping missions.

In regard to South Africa, much has been expected of her since she achieved majority rule in 1994, in virtually every area of government, both by the international community and by the African states themselves. Certainly at the outset, President Nelson Mandela wanted to promote peace and stability on his own continent but envisaged achieving this by way of negotiation and 'preventive diplomacy' rather than active military involvement. In 1996 Tanzania and

Mozambique requested naval support from South Africa in keeping their fishing grounds free of poachers, but these requests, slight in themselves, were refused by Mandela. Likewise in 1998, when Zimbabwe, Angola and Namibia were contemplating intervention in Congo in support of the Laurent Kabila government, they requested that South Africa should join them, a request which was again refused. In neither case did Mandela see South Africa's interests as being directly involved, and it was not until September 1998, when the Mosisili government in Lesotho was coming under pressure from dissident internal elements, that President Mandela intervened in support of it along with Botswana.[11] His reasons for doing so were twofold: he feared that violence in Lesotho might 'spill over' and affect South Africa itself and he wanted furthermore to ensure the safety of the Lesotho Highlands Water Project on which South Africa relied for a good part of its water supply. This intervention was actually approved by SADC as a whole, even though only Botswana actively supported it, but Mandela's refusal shortly beforehand to participate in the Congo intervention did not endear him to Zimbabwe, Angola or Namibia, who worked thereafter to minimise South African influence in SADC councils. Shortly after this successful intervention in Lesotho, the South African government published a White Paper expressing its support for the principle of peace missions backed by military force, which seemed only to rub salt into the wounds of these three SADC members.

In defence of South Africa's attitude to active military support of peace missions, it needs to be remembered that its defence budget has been cut by some 40 per cent since 1994, which has had a severe impact on both the quality and the quantity of military hardware available. Since 1994, too, many experienced officers have been retired or have accepted redundancy packages so that the requisite expertise at senior level is simply not available. The average age of serving military personnel in the South African Defence Forces (SADF) is now 38 and approximately 25 per cent of them are affected by AIDS.[12] This does not, in sum, make for a very impressive military force and it has been reliably estimated that it will be at least a decade before the SADF are in a position to undertake support operations under Chapter VII of the UN Charter.

This situation must inevitably affect Pretoria's attitude to involvement in military operations where shots are likely to be fired in anger. With lesser operations (of a Chapter VI nature) they will probably be able to cope, but not comfortably, and it will probably take five years for the situation to ease.[13] Currently, South Africa is active on the ground in the Democratic Republic of Congo (DRC), Burundi, Rwanda and the Sudan, but the commitments are not massive and the numbers involved are small: for example, there are only 1,400 South African personnel in the vast territory of DRC and 240 in Burundi, reduced from an original 700.

That said, there can be no doubt about Mbeki's intention of making NEPAD work – with all its implications for peacekeeping and 'peace-missioning' generally. In 2001, he stated his determination that the twenty-first century should be 'Africa's century' and indeed results to date have not been unimpressive. Over 2000–4 Mbeki actively pursued a diplomatic role in the Great Lakes region, trying to secure a peace settlement in the DRC with the assistance of Deputy-President Jacob Zuma, who negotiated the withdrawal of all Rwandan forces from DRC and, with SADC approval, consolidated the government of Joseph Kabila, son of the assassinated Laurent. Likewise, he poured oil on troubled waters in Uganda and the Sudan during this period, winding down a situation in which both governments were supporting dissident elements in one another's countries. Slightly earlier, over 1999–2001, ex-president Mandela and Jacob Zuma successfully negotiated an arrangement for Burundi, whereby during the next three years to 2004, Hutus and Tutsis would alternate in the offices of president and vice-president respectively, thereby ensuring that both the major tribes had a political stake in that unhappy country. South Africa provided a peacekeeping force of 700 personnel to monitor the arrangement, a force which remains in place today, albeit at a reduced level. She also played a significant diplomatic role in engineering the peace treaty between the Arab north and the African south in the Sudan which was finally put in place in January 2005.

These are substantial achievements and reflect well on Mbeki. However, he has fought shy of becoming overstretched in military terms and refused a suggestion from Angola's president, Dos Santos, to provide his MPLA government with assistance in the war against Savimbi's UNITA in the 2000–2 period. He thereby incurred the displeasure not only of Dos Santos but of Presidents Mugabe and Nujoma as well, Zimbabwe and Namibia being in broad alliance with Angola. His calculation that South Africa could not safely get involved in the Angolan imbroglio was almost certainly a wise one, but the question of whether or not to intervene in a particular scenario is always politically delicate and likely to cause controversy whichever decision is reached. This is not a problem likely to just go away.

## The Southern African Development Community (SADC)

SADC was formed in 1992 by the Treaty of Windhoek out of the former Southern African Development Co-ordinating Conference, established in 1980, to relieve its economic dependence on the Republic of South Africa. It was joined in 1994 by the latter after its accession to majority rule in May of that year: this was welcomed by its member states as well as by South Africa itself.

South Africa's position within the organisation was unique, in that its economic wealth, resources and population dwarfed those of the other ten member states and placed it in the position of being a pivotal, if not indeed hegemonic, state. This was not a situation it had either coveted or sought and it did give rise to difficult economic and diplomatic relations with its northern neighbours, who expected it to contribute generously to the community but to accept a self-denying ordinance as far as its own economic and political aspirations were concerned. This was not perhaps a situation which could long endure: South Africa appreciated this very well and in the years after 1994 did its best to avert situations in which the charge of 'hegemon' could be raised against it. Diplomatically, this was far from easy.

The other members of SADC remembered all too well the heyday of apartheid in the 1970s and the 'destabilisation' policy of P.W. Botha's South Africa in the 1980s and regarded the new South Africa with apprehension and mistrust, notwithstanding the fact of 'regime change'. Would the new South Africa try to be as dominant as its predecessor had been domineering?

The first clash came in 1995 over the issue of sanctions against Nigeria following the execution of Ken Saro-Wiwa and his Ogoni colleagues.[14] This execution had taken place abruptly following the trial of the accused for murder before a military tribunal in camera: it had for the regime immensely political overtones and there is no doubt that the tribunal was under severe pressure to convict. The issue was complicated by the factor of Commonwealth politics, in that both Mandela and the Commonwealth secretary-general had put in pleas for clemency: these were disregarded and the executions went ahead and were announced on the first day of the CHOGM in Auckland, New Zealand. Nigeria was suspended from Commonwealth membership and a furious Mandela also proposed to SADC that it should itself take economic sanctions against Nigeria. This was refused by the totality of SADC governments in a vote which implied that the matter was purely internal to Nigeria and not one in which SADC should be expected to involve itself or, by implication, the Commonwealth. The outcome was a distinct slap in the face for President Mandela.

The second clash of opinion came in 1996 between President Mandela of South Africa and President Mugabe of Zimbabwe. The issue was who or what should have final control over SADC security: the Organ of Policy, Defence and Security (OPDS) collectively or its chairman, President Mugabe, who had been in this post since 1992. The latter had succeeded since then in asserting a certain dominance in security policy, but in 1996 Mandela argued against SADC intervening qua SADC in the civil conflict in DRC. Mugabe said that South Africa should do his bidding as OPDS chairman, but Mandela disagreed, saying that intervention should be a matter for collective decision by the organ, and refused to comply. The result was a rift between the two men which lasted for the duration of Mandela's presidency and affected South African–Zimbabwean bilateral relations thereafter. Mandela's motive for reaching this decision was partly political, in that it was for DRC to determine who ruled in Kinshasha, and, partly, military and strategic in that he doubted whether South Africa could cope with the degree of intervention which such a scenario would require.

The third incident involved South Africa's positive response to a joint request from the USA and the EU in 1999 that it should sign an economic and trading agreement with them. The problem was that this invitation did not include the other members of SADC: South Africa's unilateral acceptance of it without consulting the other members was taken by them as a distinct slight and served only to strengthen the general feelings in the community that, at heart, South Africa was 'hegemonic', if not indeed 'pro-West' and enjoyed a privileged type of membership in which consultation with colleagues was not deemed to be necessary. When one considers the extent of President Mandela's negotiating and diplomatic skills, so frequently manifest since 1990, this was an extraordinarily insensitive démarche and one only to be explained by the advantages he perceived would accrue from it to South Africa: it was hardly *communautaire*.

This raises, of course, the whole question of how far international organisations can be genuinely dispassionate when faced with cogent issues of national politics. There is, for example, considerable nationalist thinking apparent all the time in the EU institutions in Brussels: in January 1963, Couve de Murville, then France's foreign secretary, vetoed Britain's first application to join what was then the European Economic Community on the orders of President de Gaulle, because to do otherwise would have been contrary to the interests of French farmers and hence to de Gaulle's own electoral survival, despite an almost universal wish in the EEC at that time that the UK should be admitted. Likewise in 1999, Mandela was in a position to ride roughshod over the other members of SADC and there was little they could do about it. They lacked the requisite clout as had the other five member states of the EEC in 1963.

This raises further considerations which, however interesting, are too controversial to explore in fine detail. The first is that South Africa (and Nigeria, in an ECOWAS context) needs to act like a hegemon if Africa is going to rise like a phoenix from the ashes and make NEPAD and the African Renaissance a reality; otherwise everything will turn to dust.[15] Secondly, by the same token, the smaller states of SADC are going to have to accept a subordinate status in the interim for the greater good of the whole. That will require of them, politically, a considerable effort of the soul.

## The Zimbabwe issue

Of all the current issues of foreign policy in Southern Africa, that of Zimbabwe has proved the most vexatious and the most intractable. It has had a major impact on the region in general and on South Africa in particular, as events in Zimbabwe during the last decade and especially since 2000 have run completely counter to all the principles of good governance NEPAD has been trying to foster and to which President Thabo Mbeki has been so personally committed. The question has inevitably been raised, especially in Western international circles, as to why South Africa has been so slow in addressing the problem by exerting diplomatic or economic pressure on Zimbabwe.

To answer this question, it is really necessary to return to the early 1990s. In 1990, Nelson Mandela was released from prison and in 1994 became leader of South Africa, now under majority rule. His release and subsequent accession to the presidency immediately caused the political spotlight to shift onto him at the expense of Robert Mugabe. This did not please the latter, who was visibly taken aback at the warmth of the welcome accorded to Mandela in Zimbabwe when he paid his first official visit there in June 1994: the plaudits Mandela then received from ordinary Zimbabweans far exceeded those bestowed upon Mugabe as head of state. This marked the start of a relationship already rather diplomatically brittle, as during the war of liberation in the 1980s Mugabe had tended to favour the Pan-African Congress (PAC) rather than Mandela's ANC. In 1996, furthermore, there was open disagreement between the two presidents over how the SADC Organ on Policy, Defence and Security should operate and who should have ultimate control.[16] This increased the resentment already felt by Mugabe which survived the Mandela presidency and affected his relationship with Mbeki. The latter, however, did not want to press Mugabe too far, partly because he needed Zimbabwe's political support – or at least her acquiescence – within SADC councils and partly because he wanted to have some leverage over the course of the war in the DRC. It was also the case that the 1997 ANC party conference had enjoined the government to strengthen South Africa's ties with the 'liberation parties' in the region, which, of course, included ZANU-PF.

These various considerations all served to dissuade Mbeki, not one by temperament for confrontation in any case, from standing up to Mugabe – even after his behaviour on land policy worsened following his defeat in the 2000 referendum on the Constitution. But this was not all. The collective membership of SADC did not view Mugabe's policy as rapacious, illegal or affronting human rights but rather as 'unfinished colonial business' and, as such, a matter for the Zimbabwean government. Only President Festus Mogae of Botswana actually condemned Mugabe in public, whilst Mbeki, whatever he might have said to Mugabe in private, was publicly silent on the issue. This silence has served in recent years to diminish both the political stature of South Africa as a state committed to democracy, human rights and the rule of law and the credibility of NEPAD as an organisation which can, when push comes to shove, deliver Africa from its own excesses.

Whilst Mbeki and indeed SADC too should be condemned for their failure to confront Zimbabwe by way of sanctions or diplomatic pressure, it should also be remembered that Mugabe, as a former anti-colonial fighter for the liberation of Rhodesia, does enjoy very considerable popularity amongst the South African masses even if its professional and business community regard his behaviour as highly reprehensible. However, the South African masses, for the most part poverty-stricken and unemployed, see Robert Mugabe as their protagonist and the acclaim he received in 2004 when he visited Pretoria for the tenth anniversary of South Africa's accession to majority rule was not in scale dissimilar to that given to Nelson Mandela when he visited Harare in 1994. This does not bode well for the future of good governance in Southern Africa.

Mbeki, furthermore, has other – and less creditable – reasons for pussyfooting over policy in Zimbabwe. Despite the pleas made to him by Morgan Tsvangirai's MDC for support in righting the injustices of Zimbabwe's situation, these pleas have fallen on deaf ears. Firstly, Mbeki is fearful that the success of the MDC in Zimbabwe, an opposition party emanating from the trade union movement, could trigger an accretion of support to the Confederation of South African Trade Unions (COSATU) in his own country and conceivably undermine the tripartite alliance of the ANC, the SACP and COSATU on which his own political power rests. It is better, therefore, to have Mugabe in power, disreputable though he is, than to have Tsvangirai sharing power with him in coalition with all the uncertainty that might create for the political balance in South Africa itself. Secondly, Mbeki is apprehensive that any worsening of the law-and-order situation in Zimbabwe or possibly even incipient anarchy there would cause an increase in the number of 'economic' migrants (of which the flow is already considerable) entering South Africa and exacerbating existing tensions amongst the indigenous population. There would also be a threat to the considerable South African commercial investments in Zimbabwe in the event of yet greater uncertainty or general collapse and Mbeki does not want to take any action, however justified in terms of human rights or good governance, which might precipitate such a situation. Thirdly, given that SADC as a whole does not want to condemn Mugabe, Mbeki hesitates to confront him on his own and derogate thereby from African political unity. There is little doubt that he could make life very difficult for Zimbabwe if he so chose, but for all these various reasons he does not for the moment 'choose' and just how long this situation will persist must remain a matter for conjecture.

## Liberation and reform politics

These two very different kinds of politics impact on the domestic as well as the foreign policy scene and are most appropriately described as mutually antagonistic political cultures which crucially affect government attitudes over a wide range of issues – respect for human rights and the rule of law, the doctrine of state sovereignty, the Zimbabwe issue and the implementation of NEPAD principles continent-wide. Whether a state belongs to the liberation or the reform camp is, in the context of these matters, highly significant.

Prior to the collapse of White rule in the various countries of the region, all the African political parties were, by definition, pursuing liberation politics in their attempts to destroy that rule. That was indeed the only item on their agenda because, unless this was done, nothing else could be. In Angola, Mozambique, Zimbabwe and Namibia, the struggle was long and bitter, although in the end successful. During this time, the leaders of these African nationalist parties developed a certain mindset in their dealings with White power, a mindset based on irredentism and determination to overthrow it. Self-government was good: anything else was unacceptable and to achieve self-government anything was permitted.

The problem was (and is) that this attitude to White economic and political power survived the latter's demise in the 1980s and 1990s in a number of Southern African states. This has made for a certain ruthlessness and arbitrariness in the way they reach important political decisions and indeed in their whole attitude to government. They want solutions and they want them now: due process and constitutional niceties, however desirable for dressing the windows of politics, are in the final analysis less important than achieving the main strategic goals. During colonial times, these were achieved not by treaties, agreements and due process but by blood and fire. In Southern Africa, the countries which broadly adhere to this line, seven years into the twenty-first century, are Zimbabwe, Angola, Namibia and arguably Swaziland. Of these, Zimbabwe has behaved sufficiently badly as to place it for many countries in the international community (though not in the African) in the category of 'rogue state'. It has involved itself, along with Angola and Namibia, in the Congolese war for reasons of economic self-interest. Angola and Namibia, whilst certainly not in the same category, have yet to exhibit a genuine and continuing respect for due process and the rule of law. Namibia, far from condemning Zimbabwe's policies on land acquisition, shows signs of moving in a similar direction itself and in recent years has indicated considerable hostility to journalists who have criticised politics emanating from Windhoek. Overall, however, it has acted in a constitutional and open-handed manner. Angola, whilst it emerged more successfully from its civil war in 2002 than many dared to hope, has still to develop sufficient transparency in its economic and political infrastructure and to ensure that its 'over-mighty' barons operate within – and not beyond – the rule of law.[17] Swaziland, with its absolute monarchy, is rather in a category of its own in regard to political governance, the king being regarded by his subjects as almost divine in status.

However, by no means all the states of Southern Africa espouse liberation politics. Botswana, Mozambique, Lesotho and South Africa are all 'reformers'. Botswana, in particular, has adhered strictly to both the letter and the spirit of its Constitution and, notwithstanding the overwhelming size of the governing party, has ensured the maintenance of a 'level playing field' on which all politics may joust. President Festus Mogae alone of all his counterparts in SADC has publicly condemned President Mugabe's regime for its many derogations from human rights.

Mozambique has performed similarly in recent years under President Chissano, RENAMO having successfully completed the transition – for the moment at any rate – from guerrilla organisation to constitutional opposition party. Lesotho's situation is rather less certain, though it does appear that the Mosisili government, itself popularly elected in 1998, has succeeded in establishing a stable and decent polity after the upheavals of the period 1999–2003. Its anti-corruption record has certainly been impressive[18] and hopefully will be emulated by the other states of SADC.

South Africa, under Thabo Mbeki, is firmly within the reform camp. This is evidenced by his continuing concern for the NEPAD programme to be adopted by as many African states as possible and he has been well assisted in this by Presidents Obasanjo and Bouteflika of Nigeria and Algeria respectively. Though he has not condemned his neighbour President Mugabe's land policies, as most believe he should have done, he has not allowed illegal and arbitrary land seizures to take place within South Africa itself, nor stood aside from combating corruption in high places, as his dismissal of Jacob Zuma from the deputy-presidency in 2005 showed. That said, it should not be forgotten that he presides over a party which is a 'very broad church'. There are many in the ANC who would like the government to drink more deeply at the springs of 'liberation politics' than Mbeki is prepared to do and to return to the more 'ethical' foreign policy of his illustrious predecessor, even if this involves greater risk of diplomatic conflict with the West and the G8. This is not, of course, the view of the main opposition party, the Democratic Alliance, which has on a number of occasions criticised the ANC in parliament when it sees some of its members as veering down the 'liberation politics' road. However, Mbeki's government has, to its credit, not gone down that road.

The divide between the liberators and the reformers, however, is not confined to Southern Africa. It extends over the whole continent and is particularly notable in the councils of NEPAD. The latter's Implementation Committee, established in 2003 to monitor performance towards its main objectives, consists of six members: President Yar'Adua (succeeding President Obasanjo; Nigeria), Thabo Mbeki (South Africa), Abdulaziz Bouteflika (Algeria), Muammar Gaddafi (Libya), Paul Biya (Cameroon) and Omar Bongo (Gabon). Whilst the first three named have been active in the establishment of NEPAD and are, by nature, 'reform' politicians anxious to find consensus, the same cannot be said of the last three, who adhere to the doctrine of 'absolute state sovereignty' and whose ideas include the early establishment of a United States of Africa and a pan-continental army. Their presence on the committee has, in the last three years, not assisted progress. The result has been a certain degree of diplomatic friction between these two groups and hence the slower achievement of NEPAD objectives than might have been. Ultimately, this whole matter may well turn on how far Nigeria and South Africa can forge an irresistible alliance strong enough to drive the continent economically and politically forward, irrespective of the charges of 'hegemon' which may be laid against both of them.

# 5　Conclusions

We are now almost at the end of our analytical journey through Southern Africa and the time has come to draw what conclusions we may. However, we must throughout bear in mind the scope of the political changes that have occurred in the region in the last four decades and particularly in the last two. The joke common in the airline industry in the 1960s and 1970s that on arrival at any of the Southern African capitals passengers should be advised to put back their watches 50 years is no longer apt.

On the economic front, the changes have been much less notable than on the political. The countries' wealth and natural resources tend to be concentrated, as before, in the hands of the Whites, even if the Asian community in South Africa is strongly challenging this European economic dominance. There is a growing Black economic elite in South Africa, though at the time of writing it remains small. Throughout the region, African impoverishment and unemployment continue to be very marked, especially beyond the borders of South Africa. Even in South Africa itself, employment remains at an unacceptably high level with 26 per cent of the Black workforce officially unemployed and approximately 40 per cent in fact unemployed due to the vagaries of the informal economy. It is difficult to be definitive about this, but what is certain is that this large and growing pool of Black unemployment constitutes a long-term threat to the well-being of South Africa,[1] and its economy needs, in future, to grow at the rate of 6 per cent rather than its present 4.5 per cent if this problem is to be adequately addressed. The accelerated and shared growth initiative (ASGI) established by the government in 2005 will hopefully make an impact on expanding the economy, though there is a fear that poor delivery service and too strong a rand may diminish that impact. Although the ANC government has managed the economy satisfactorily since 1994 in terms of reducing both the rate of inflation and the public debt, it has failed, as yet, to attract the amount of foreign direct investment it had hoped for in 1994. The causes of this are several, but the alarming rates of crime and violence in South Africa and the failure of Pretoria to address the problem of Zimbabwe convincingly are almost certainly amongst them; at present, there are little grounds for optimism on either front.

Whilst 'Black empowerment' is seen by many as a legitimate 'fast track' to African prosperity, two dangers to this course of action present themselves. The first is the temptation to recruit Africans into jobs for which they do not have adequate education and training: the period 1976–89 resulted in an efflux of many youngsters to territories north of the River Limpopo to fight with the ANC's army of liberation and as a result, years of education were lost, leaving South Africa today with a severe shortage of skills especially in the building, engineering, plumbing and electrical trades.[2] The recruitment of unqualified people has inevitably caused problems over the efficient execution of work, although steps are currently being taken to address this problem through government-financed 'skills-development' courses. The second danger is significant White emigration because they consider they now have little long-term future in their own country. And yet South Africa needs all the skills it can get, White as well as Black. The way forward is to open up every opportunity for the latter but only once they are properly qualified. However, in view of the long history of Black deprivation, this may not be feasible politically. What is crucial is for government to provide a base from which Blacks can on their own move upwards in socio-economic terms as far as their ability and industry will carry them. This applies equally to South Africa's neighbours, though this is sadly more difficult for them to achieve due to their smaller and less sophisticated economies and to a yet more parlous employment situation.

On the political front, what must above all be striven for is stability and constitutional governance. The latter, if implemented, will promote the former and this will, in turn, encourage the inflow of foreign direct investment upon which the prosperity of the whole region so much depends. Only in Zimbabwe is the present picture black as jet: in all the other countries, even Swaziland, there are the trappings of constitutionality though actual performance between them does vary considerably. Angola and Namibia have advanced less far down the democratic road than Mozambique and Botswana: in Angola, there continue to be 'overmighty barons' who are able to operate outside the framework of law, notably in regard to oil, tax and land, and in Namibia, members of the media who are too overtly and effectively critical tend to come in for governmental harassment. Also, the Namibian government's benign attitude towards the regime of President Mugabe remains a cause for concern. The appeal of 'liberation politics' is far from dead in Harare, Luanda or Windhoek. However, in Mozambique, Botswana, Lesotho and South Africa itself, 'reform politics' remains the norm even if there are occasional wrinkles on the canvas of constitutional government.

By 'wrinkles', I mean derelictions from due process, minority rights and the spirit of democracy. Whilst the record of Botswana's government is second to none in terms of governance, the San and Bushmen peoples would probably feel that the government could and should have treated them with more consideration in the matter of continued possession of their ancestral land. In Mozambique, democracy is equated with more prosperity and less unemployment; things like 'due process of law' remain something of a closed book, notwithstanding that this is the essence of constitutional government. In South Africa, the African National Congress dominates Parliament and accepts the Democratic Alliance as the official opposition and the other much smaller parties as adherents to it. But would it accept the Democratic Alliance so readily, if it were running the government neck-and-neck electorally? The answer is probably 'no': both Tony Leon, the DA's leader until May 2007, and Helen Suzman have in the recent past been castigated as 'closet supporters of apartheid' by elements of the ANC simply because they happened to be MPs during the apartheid era. Since 1994, the ANC government has reduced the parliamentary time available for questioning of their policies and activities to a level well below that available in the apartheid era and has also attempted, sometimes successfully, to detach MPs from the Democratic Alliance by the offer of jobs and other inducements. Behaviour and remarks of this kind do give cause for concern as to the ANC's underlying 'democratic spirit', a concern much reinforced by the system of iron discipline, Lenin-style, by which the ANC in parliament is managed. I accept the comment sometimes heard in South Africa that the ANC possesses a democratic body, but not a democratic soul. The concept of 'loyal opposition' has yet to be fully understood and appreciated throughout Southern Africa, including South Africa.

Security is so multi-faceted that it jostles with both economic and political concerns. The AIDS pandemic affecting the whole region has impacted on state economies enormously (which is why it is considered in the first chapter of this book). It has contributed greatly to people's sense of insecurity by eliminating breadwinners and leaving mothers and children to cope on their own: sometimes it has eliminated both parents, throwing the responsibility of the children onto elderly grandparents. It has resulted in mass absenteeism from both the school and the workplace and attendance at funerals is extremely common. Immigration, which basically involves South Africa, contributes to insecurity in numerous ways. The immigrants arrive in a country they do not know and then have to find work, which in rural areas is often badly paid or not to be had. As many of them arrive illegally, they are liable to come to the attention of the police and the indigenous population, who greatly resent their presence because it depresses wage levels and tend to bully them in consequence. If they tangle with the police, the police treat them badly or accept bribes for 'turning a blind eye'. Nobody knows the precise rate of migrant inflow from the territories north of the Limpopo, but 200,000 per month has been mentioned and the numbers of people in South Africa illegally is of the order of five million, possibly more. South Africa will need to address the reasons for this inflow and endeavour to stem it. However, the only way for it to achieve this in any permanent sense is to encourage, via SADC, a greater spread of development – and employment – in the countries to its north.

More generally, there is throughout the region a certain cult of brutality and violence.[3] This dates back to the apartheid period but has sadly survived it: robbery with violence is today a common occurrence and a massive home-security industry has been developed to combat it. The ordinary police have been overwhelmed by the problem and, moreover, become to varying degrees corrupt due to low pay, which diminishes their sense of stake in the system. Menfolk, too, brutalise their womenfolk to a considerable extent and rape, both within settled relationships and outside them, is distressingly common. A brooding 'fear of the other' stalks the land – not only South Africa, but the region generally. If it is to develop happily, this fear must be assuaged and positive political leadership both in this matter and in that of eliminating police corruption is called for.

With concern to foreign policy, South Africa's position in Southern Africa will always remain pivotal in view of its size and wealth, but it is unlikely for the foreseeable future to be in a position to dominate. This is partly because it does not wish to and partly because it realises that any attempt at 'hegemony' would be resented by its SADC partners. As things are, it is seen by the latter as too conservative and 'Western-orientated' because of its orthodox, free-market economic policy, and yet, paradoxically, it needs to 'exercise hegemony' to a considerable extent if the region is to prosper over time and the smaller states of SADC should realise and accept this. I do not believe, however, that they are likely to do so because of the strength of their individual nationalisms and because of the suspicion and fear in which they have historically held South Africa. If I am right, SADC will, therefore, be less effective as an economic and political organisation than otherwise it might be.

That said – and again paradoxically – Southern Africa will continue to expect much from South Africa, as from an indulgent father, but will baulk if that same father becomes even slightly reproving. This is clearly an untenable situation for South Africa and one unlikely to endure. The challenge for South Africa will be to exercise an unobtrusive leadership within SADC, encouraging through carrots rather than sticks the cooperation of its other members over policies prompted by itself. In this regard, any future South African president should endeavour to emulate the pragmatism of a Thabo Mbeki rather than the mercurialism of a Nelson Mandela. South Africa, too, however much it wishes to consider Southern Africa and, beyond that, Africa generally, can hardly be expected to do so at the expense of its own national interests and massive domestic problems.

Though NEPAD and the AU go beyond the geopolitical scope of Southern Africa, it is hard to see how South Africa can be other than closely bound up with their respective destinies even if the other members of SADC may not be. Progress for both organisations is likely to depend on the potency of individual state nationalism, which is currently not to be underrated. The withholding of AU subscriptions by Algeria, Nigeria, Libya and Egypt in protest at the siting of the proposed African parliament at Gauteng in South Africa is petty and does not bode well for that organisation's future: relatively little positive interest too has been shown in NEPAD outside South Africa and Nigeria, the efforts of their two presidents notwithstanding. It may well be that only a strong political and diplomatic alliance between Mbeki and Yar'Adua will enable both organisations to set Southern Africa – and Africa generally – on a road leading out of poverty and misgovernance towards a genuine African renaissance.

What conclusions, finally, can be drawn about Southern Africa? No one can deny – and certainly I do not – that immense problems remain. HIV/AIDS bedevils the whole region, accounting for much waste, misery and loss of life. Insecurity in general – especially violence against women – is endemic and few feel genuinely free in either body or goods. Only a minority of people have secure and reasonably remunerated employment and most of these are male and White: genuine reconciliation across the colour line will much depend on the degree and pace of economic restitution. Immigration from north to south across the porous frontiers of South Africa causes immense socio-economic problems for that country and the failure of SADC in general and of South Africa in particular to address the injustice of the situation in Zimbabwe diminishes the international respect in which Southern Africa is currently held. SADC and NEPAD are unlikely to make a great impact on this or other foreign policy scenarios because of the continuing strength of the individual nationalisms but, as international organisations, it is nevertheless right that they should assert themselves to the full against absolutist sovereign states. However, notwithstanding these difficulties, a massive sea change has occurred in the last three decades. Majority, not minority, rule is now in place and has been brought about more peacefully than most people dared to hope. Even though it will probably be many a year before the region as a whole reaches 'the broad, sunlit uplands' of general prosperity and reconciliation, a start has at least been made. Racial discrimination and the oppression this occasioned for so many throughout the region are now things of the past. Provided that constitutional governance and due process of law become the norm – provided, in other words, that 'reform politics' eventually prevails over 'liberation politics' – then, and only then, will those sunlit uplands beckon.

# Notes

## 1 The economic and social dimension

1 P. Keatley, *The Politics of Partnership*, Harmondsworth: Penguin, 1963, Part IV, Chapter 3, p. 275.
2 The Mines and Works Amendment Act, 1926.
3 See A. Sparks, *The Mind of South Africa*, London: Mandarin, 1991, p. 194.
4 These policies demanded, except in the smallest of firms, that a certain proportion of 'civilised' (i.e. White) labour had to be recruited before any 'uncivilised' (i.e. non-White) labour could be employed at all.
5 See A. Butler, *Contemporary South Africa*, Basingstoke: Palgrave Macmillan, 2004, p. 15.
6 See Chapter 2, pp. 53–4.
7 See N. Mandela, *Long Walk to Freedom*, Boston: Little, Brown and Co., 1994, pp. 163–4.
8 See M. Gorbachev, *Perestroika: New Thinking for Our Country and the World*, New York and London: Harper and Row, 1987, Chapter 1, pp. 45–59.
9 See p. 9.
10 N. Vink, 'Patience Running Out: Land Reform', *The World Today* (Royal Institute of International Affairs) March 2004, pp. 21–3.
11 For a full account of these and other activities, see Rio Tinto PLC archives, Articles 38 and 39 ref. ARD/4.
12 See S. Kell and T. Dyer, 'Economic Integration in South Africa', in Y. Bradshaw and S.N. Ndegwa (eds), *The Uncertain Promise of Southern Africa*, Bloomington: Indiana University Press, 2000, Chapter 14, pp. 363–89.
13 World Bank, *African Development Indicators*, 2002.
14 E. Kalipeni, 'Health and Society in Southern Africa in Times of Economic Turbulence', in Bradshaw and Ndegwa, *Uncertain Promise*, pp. 350–5.
15 South Africa is currently spending some 30 per cent of her budget on these items and 20 per cent on debt servicing. S. Benatar, 'South Africa's Transition in a Globalising World', *International Affairs* (Royal Institute of International Affairs), April 2001, pp. 356–8.
16 Nana Poku, 'Poverty, Debt and Africa's HIV/AIDS Crisis', *International Affairs* (Royal Institute of International Affairs), July 2002, pp. 530–46.

17  Report of Zambia Demographic Visit, University of Malawi, 1991.
18  See H. Deegan, *South Africa Reborn: Building a New Democracy*, London: UCL Press, 1998, p. 83.
19  See Butler, *Contemporary South Africa*, p. 84.

## 2  The political dimension

1   See Chapter 1, pp. 10–12.
2   Within the Nationalist Party, Hendrick Verwoerd, later South African prime minister 1958–66, was perhaps apartheid's leading philosophical protagonist.
3   For a fuller account, see Chapter 3, pp. 106–8.
4   See Helen Suzman's autobiography *In No Uncertain Terms: Memoirs*, London: Sinclair Stevenson, 1993, pp. 113–15.
5   Keatley, *Politics of Partnership*, Part Four, Chapter 4, pp. 314–17.
6   See Judith Todd's autobiography, *The Right to Say No*, Harare: Longman Zimbabwe, 1987.
7   For a more detailed account, see J. Duffy's *Portuguese Africa*, Cambridge, MA: Harvard University Press, 1959, Chapter 11, pp. 268–78.
8   Ibid., Chapter 11.
9   P.L. Moorcraft, *African Nemesis: War and Revolution in Southern Africa*, London: Brassey's, 1990, Chapters 5–8.
10  Sparks, *The Mind of South Africa*, Chapter 15, p. 226.
11  See Chapter 4, p. 119.
12  These elections indicated 49.6 per cent for Dos Santos and 40.1 per cent for Savimbi, the remaining 11.3 per cent of the vote going to several other candidates.
13  It is of note that Savimbi did not personally sign the Protocol but sent a representative, E. Mannvakolic, whose signature he later repudiated.
14  For a fuller account of this period, see Tony Hodges, *Angola: Anatomy of an Oil State*, Oxford: Fridtjof Nansen Institute in assocation with James Currey, 2004, Chapter 1, pp. 9–19.
15  One of these, the UNITA-Renovado, actually went into alliance with the MPLA.
16  Agricultural output declined from 50 per cent to 17 per cent of Angolan GDP between 1960 and 1995.
17  Most of these people have since 2002 returned to their region of origin, though a number remain outside the country awaiting repatriation.
18  This view is reflected in the report of the UN Development Programme of May 2004.
19  See *Angola Peace Monitor* 9(10), June 2004, published by Action for Southern Africa (ACTSA).
20  See its 1997 report on political participation and human rights in Southern Africa.
21  In 1982, 524,000 tons of cereal had to be imported; in 1974, Mozambique had been self-sufficient in cereals. Bradshaw and Ndegwa, *Uncertain Promise*, p. 190.
22  Mozambique's economy declined as a result of these activities by 8 per cent during 1980–5. See Paul Nugent, *Africa since Independence*, Basingstoke: Palgrave Macmillan, 2004, p. 285.

23 See pp. 55–6.
24 See Bradshaw and Ndegwa, *Uncertain Promise*, pp. 188–207.
25 Currently, Mozambique's budget is supported to the tune of 50 per cent by outside donors.
26 In these elections, the presidential pollings were 52.3 per cent for Chissano and 47.7 per cent for Dhlakama.
27 EU observers did report, however, that 'serious irregularities' occurred during these elections.
28 The Presidential Powers (Temporary Powers) Act enabled Mugabe to amend the Land Acquisition Act of 1992 unilaterally.
29 This torture was subsequently admitted in court by the police commissioner under cross-examination.
30 This included John Howard of Australia, Olusegun Obasanjo of Nigeria and Thabo Mbeki of South Africa.
31 Much of this evidence consisted of an audio-tape recording of a conversation between Tsvangirai and a Canadian journalist in which the former was alleged to have been planning the assassination of Mugabe. Not only was the soundtrack very poor but the journalist concerned admitted to accepting money from the Zimbabwe government.
32 Twelve of the Commonwealth states of Southern Africa dissociated themselves from this decision.
33 Such legislation as the Law and Order Maintenance Act (1960) under which both Mugabe and Nkomo were imprisoned in 1963 remained in place – and was deployed on numerous occasions.
34 This was the distinct impression gained during private conversations in Harare in 1995.
35 T.E. Ranger, 'Cultural Revolution', *The World Today* (Royal Institute of International Affairs) Feb. 2002, pp. 23–5.
36 Lines written by William Wordsworth in 1790 on the success of the French Revolution.
37 TRC formally disbanded in July 1998. But its work continued after that date under a new name, the Institute of Change, Memory and Reconciliation, with Archbishop Tutu as chairman.
38 Alex Boraine, *A Country Unmasked: Inside South Africa's Truth and Reconciliation Commission*, Cape Town and Oxford: Oxford University Press, 2004, Chapter 10, pp. 340–78.
39 Ibid., p. 352.
40 For further information on the TRC, see Steven Gish, *Desmond Tutu: A Biography*, Westport, CT: Greenwood Press, 2004, pp. 147–61.
41 The death penalty was also declared unconstitutional by the Constitutional Court in 1995 and abolished.
42 Of the 11 judges on the Constitutional Court, only four are legal experts emanating from the South African bench: the remaining seven appointments are at presidential discretion on the basis of his assessment of their 'stand in the community' and 'contribution to public life'.
43 Formerly South Africa ambassador in London between 1984 and 1989. He then resigned to go into domestic politics.
44 30 per cent transfer of White farmland promised in 1994; by 2004, only 2 per cent actually transferred.
45 *The World Factbook – Botswana* 2004.

46  The government had to cope with serious rioting in Gaberone in 1987 in protest at the extent of unemployment.
47  In Swazi traditional custom, the throne reverts to the 'great she-elephant', the mother to the heir to the throne, if the latter is not yet of age.
48  33.4 per cent of Swazi adults are HIV-positive, a position similar to that of South Africa.
49  South Africa has always been apprehensive that any instability in Lesotho might 'spill over' and affect its own territory.
50  Musupha Sole, chief executive of the Lesotho Highlands Water Project, was sentenced in 2002 to 18 years in prison for accepting bribes, and Schneider Electric and Lahmeyers were fined 10 and 12 million rand respectively for offering them.
51  For a fuller account of this, see J.D. Holm and S. Darnolf, 'Democratising the Administrative State in Botswana', in Bradshaw and Ndegwa, *Uncertain Promise*, Chapter 10, pp. 115–48.
52  In the 1990 elections, ZANU-PF polled 147 of the 150 parliamentary seats.
53  See pp. 65–6.
54  See pp. 97–8.
55  Zuma was formally arraigned on corruption charges in June 2005 pending his trial later in that year. See Keesings Archives 2005, vol. 51, pp. 46,671–2.

## 3  The security dimension

1  See Chapter 1, p. 8.
2  See D. Abshire and M.A. Samuels (eds), *Portuguese Africa: A Handbook*, London: Pall Mall Press, 1969, p. 103.
3  Forcible transportation from Mozambique to Angola was not unknown. See M. Newitt, *A History of Mozambique*, London: C. Hurst, 1995, pp. 412–13.
4  See Chapter 2, pp. 49–50 for a fuller account of this.
5  See Chapter 2, p. 47.
6  Keatley, *Politics of Partnership*, p. 341.
7  See L. Thompson and A. Prior, *South African Politics*, New York and London: Yale University Press, 1982, p. 211.
8  For a full account, see L. Thompson, *A History of South Africa*, New Haven, CT, and London: Yale University Press, 1990, pp. 198–200. Also R.W. Hull, *Southern Africa: Civilizations in Turmoil*, New York: New York University Press, 1982, pp. 144–7.
9  The World Bank estimated in 1998 that some 12 per cent of South Africa's population was there illegally, i.e., circa five million. Other estimates put the figure at eight million.
10  The international average is 5.5. See R.I. Rotberg and G. Mills (eds), *War and Peace in Southern Africa: Crime, Drugs, Armies, and Trade*, Washington, DC: Brookings Institution Press, 1998, p. 2.
11  G. Arnold, *The New South Africa*, Basingstoke: Macmillan, 2000, Chapter 8, p. 89.
12  See Rotberg and Mills, *War and Peace*, Chapter 1, p. 6.
13  Ibid., Chapter 8, p. 174.

### 4 The foreign policy dimension

1 See Chapter 2, pp. 43–4.
2 Resolutions of 2 and 7 November 1956 called on Britain and France to withdraw from Egypt by majorities of 63 to 5.
3 The USA specifically declined to implement sanctions on Rhodesian exports of chrome on the ground that the USSR was the only alternative source of supply.
4 See Chapter 2, pp. 54–5 for a fuller account of this period.
5 See J.E. Spence in J. Blumenfeld (ed.), *South Africa in Crisis*, London: Croom Helm for the Royal Institute for International Affairs, 1987, pp. 168–72.
6 Nelson Mandela, 'South Africa's Future Foreign Policy', *Foreign Affairs* 72(5), November/December 1993, pp. 86–7.
7 See E. Sidiropoulos (ed.), *Apartheid Past, Renaissance Future: South Africa's Foreign Policy, 1994–2004*, Johannesburg: South African Institute of International Affairs, 2004, pp. 61–84.
8 He was in fact tried and sentenced by a military tribunal meeting in camera and the result was a foregone conclusion.
9 The name of the OAU was changed to AU at the Togo Summit of July 2000.
10 J.E. Spence, 'South Africa's Foreign Policy', in Sidiropoulos, *Apartheid Past*, pp. 35–48.
11 See Chapter 2, p. 97.
12 Conversation with defence experts at the Institute of Security Studies, Pretoria, May 2006.
13 Ibid.
14 See p. 123.
15 See A. Habib and N. Selinyane, 'South Africa's Foreign Policy and a Realistic Vision of an African Century', in Sidiropoulos, *Apartheid Past*, pp. 48–60, for a full development of this argument.
16 See pp. 128–9.
17 This relates especially to proper collection and accounting for tax revenues. See Chapter 2, pp. 61–3.
18 See Chapter 2, pp. 97–8.

### 5 Conclusions

1 This is mitigated by the fact that a quarter of the population now receive a welfare benefit of some kind.
2 For many years, mathematics was not taught at all in government schools attended by Africans.
3 See Chapter 3, pp. 108–13.

# Select bibliography

**General/historical/biographical**

Arnold, G., *The New South Africa*, Basingstoke: Macmillan, 2000

Barber, J., *South Africa in the Twentieth Century*, Oxford: Blackwell, 1999

Chan, S., *Robert Mugabe: A Life of Power and Violence*, London: I.B. Tauris, 2003

Christopher, A.J., *The Atlas of Apartheid*, London: Routledge, 1994

Clark, S. (ed.), *Nelson Mandela Speaks: Forging a Democratic Nonracial South Africa*, New York and London: Pathfinder Press, 1993

Duffy, J., *Portuguese Africa*, Cambridge, MA: Harvard University Press, 1959

Gish, S., *Desmond Tutu: A Biography*, Westport, CT: Greenwood Press, 2004

Griffiths, I.L., *The Atlas of African Affairs*, New York: Routledge, 1994

Harvey, R., *The Fall of Apartheid*, 2nd edn, Basingstoke: Palgrave Macmillan, 2003

Hull, R.W., *Southern Africa: Civilizations in Turmoil*, New York: New York University Press, 1982

Johnson, R.W., *South Africa: The First Man, The Last Nation*, London: Weidenfeld & Nicolson, 2004

Keatley, P., *The Politics of Partnership*, Harmondsworth: Penguin, 1963

Mandela, N., *Long Walk to Freedom*, Boston: Little, Brown and Co., 1994

Mbeki, T., *Africa: The Time Has Come*, Cape Town: Tafelberg, 1998

Meredith, M., *Mugabe: Power and Plunder in Zimbabwe*, New York: Public Affairs, 2003

Newitt, M., *A History of Mozambique*, London: C. Hurst, 1995

Nugent, P., *Africa since Independence*, Basingstoke: Palgrave Macmillan, 2004

Sampson, A., *Mandela: The Authorised Biography*, London: Harper Collins, 1999

Sparks, A., *The Mind of South Africa*, London: Mandarin, 1991

Suzman, H., *In No Uncertain Terms: Memoirs*, London: Sinclair Stevenson, 1993

Thompson, L., *A History of South Africa*, New Haven, CT and London: Yale University Press, 1990

Thompson, L. and Prior, A., *South African Politics*, New York and London: Yale University Press, 1982

Todd, J., *The Right to Say No*, Harare: Longman Zimbabwe, 1987
Todd, J., *Through the Darkness: A Life in Zimbabwe*, Cape Town: Zebra Press, 2007


## 1 The economic and social dimension

Abshire, D. and Samuels, M.A. (eds), *Portuguese Africa: A Handbook*, London: Pall Mall Press, 1969
Barber, J., *South Africa in the Twentieth Century*, Oxford: Blackwell, 1999
Bradshaw, Y. and Ndegwa, S.N. (eds), *The Uncertain Promise of Southern Africa*, Bloomington: Indiana University Press, 2000
Gorbachev, M., *Perestroika: New Thinking for Our Country and the World*, New York and London: Harper and Row, 1987
Hodges, T., *Angola: Anatomy of an Oil State*, Oxford: Fridtjof Nansen Institute in assocation with James Currey, 2004
Hull, R.W., *Southern Africa: Civilizations in Turmoil*, New York: New York University Press, 1982
Lessing, M. (ed.), *South African Women Today*, Cape Town: Maskew Miller Longman, 1994
Marcus, T., Eales, K. and Wildschut, A., *Down to Earth: Land Demand in the New South Africa*, Dalbridge: Indicator Press, University of Natal, 1996
Moorcraft, P.L., *African Nemesis: War and Revolution in Southern Africa*, London: Brassey's, 1990
Newitt, M., *A History of Mozambique*, London: C. Hurst, 1995
Poku, N. (ed.), *Security and Development in Southern Africa*, Westport, CT and London: Praeger Press, 2001
Sparks, A., *The Mind of South Africa*, London: Mandarin, 1991
Thompson, L., *A History of South Africa*, New Haven, CT and London: Yale University Press, 1990
Whiteside, A. and Sunter, C., *AIDS*, Cape Town: Human and Rousseau, Tafelberg, 2000


## 2 The political dimension

Boraine, A., *A Country Unmasked: Inside South Africa's Truth and Reconciliation Commission*, Cape Town and Oxford: Oxford University Press, 2004
Bradshaw, Y. and Ndegwa, S.N. (eds), *The Uncertain Promise of Southern Africa*, Bloomington: Indiana University Press, 2000
Butler, A., *Contemporary South Africa*, Basingstoke: Palgrave Macmillan, 2004
Chan, S., *Robert Mugabe: A Life of Power and Violence*, London: I.B. Tauris, 2003
Clark Leith, J., *Why Botswana Prospered*, Montreal: McGill-Queen's University Press, 2005
Deegan, H., *South Africa Reborn: Building a New Democracy*, London: UCL Press, 1998
Gish, S., *Desmond Tutu: A Biography*, Westport, CT: Greenwood Press, 2004

Gumede, W.M., *Thabo Mbeki and the Battle for the Soul of the ANC*, Cape Town: Zebra Press, 2005

Harvey, R., *The Fall of Apartheid*, 2nd edn, Basingstoke: Palgrave Macmillan, 2003

Hodges, T., *Angola: Anatomy of an Oil State*, Oxford: Fridtjof Nansen Institute in assocation with James Currey, 2004

Hull, R.W., *Southern Africa: Civilizations in Turmoil*, New York: New York University Press, 1982

Hunter-Gault, C., *New News out of Africa*, New York and Oxford: Oxford University Press, 2006

Lessing, M. (ed.), *South African Women Today*, Cape Town: Maskew Miller Longman, 1994

Lodge, T., *Consolidating Democracy: South Africa's Second Popular Election*, Johannesburg: Electoral Institute of South Africa and Witwatersrand University Press, 1999

Meredith, M., *Mugabe: Power and Plunder in Zimbabwe*, New York: Public Affairs, 2003

Nugent, P., *Africa since Independence*, Basingstoke: Palgrave Macmillan, 2004

Sparks, A., *The Mind of South Africa*, London: Mandarin, 1991

Wilson, R.A., *The Politics of Truth and Reconciliation in South Africa: Legitimizing the Post-apartheid state*, Cambridge: Cambridge University Press, 2001

### 3 The security dimension

Marcus, T., Eales, K. and Wildschut, A., *Down to Earth: Land Demand in the New South Africa*, Dalbridge: Indicator Press, University of Natal, 1996

Poku, N. (ed.), *Security and Development in Southern Africa*, Westport, CT and London: Praeger Press, 2001

Rotberg, R.I. and Mills, G. (eds), *War and Peace in Southern Africa: Crime, Drugs, Armies and Trade*, Washington, DC: Brookings Institution Press, 1998

Shaw, M., *Crime and Policing in Post-apartheid South Africa: Transforming under Fire*, London: Hurst and Co., 2002

Thompson, L., *A History of South Africa*, New Haven, CT and London: Yale University Press, 1990

Thompson, L. and Prior, A., *South African Politics*, New York and London: Yale University Press, 1982

### 4 The foreign policy dimension

Adesina, J.O., Graham, Y. and Olukoshi, A. (eds), *Africa and Development Challenges in the New Millennium: The NEPAD Debate*, Dakar: CODESRIA and London: Zed Books, 2006

Carlsnaes, W. and Muller, M. (eds), *Change and South African External Relations*, Johannesburg: International Thomson Publishing Company, 1994

Carlsnaes, W. and Nel, P. (eds), *In Full Flight: South Africa's Foreign Policy after Apartheid*, Midrand: Institute for Global Dialogue, 2006

Mills, G. (ed.), *Southern Africa into the Next Millennium*, Johannesburg: South African Institute of International Affairs, 1998

Nel, P., Taylor, I. and van der Westhuizen, J. (eds), *South Africa's Multilateral Diplomacy, and Global Change*, Aldershot: Ashgate, 2001

Sidiropoulos, E. (ed.), *Apartheid Past, Renaissance Future: South Africa's Foreign Policy, 1994–2004*, Johannesburg: South African Institute of International Affairs, 2004

Simon, D. (ed.), *South Africa in Southern Africa: Reconfiguring the Region*, Oxford: J. Currey, 1998

# Index